Riding the Demon

Riding

the Demon

On the Road in West Africa

PETER CHILSON

THE UNIVERSITY OF GEORGIA PRESS >> ATHENS AND LONDON

Published by the University of Georgia Press
Athens, Georgia 30602
© 1999 by Peter Chilson
All rights reserved
Designed by Erin Kirk New
Set in 11.5 on 14.5 Fournier
Printed and bound by Maple-Vail Book Manufacturing Group
The paper in this book meets the guidelines for permanence and durability
of the Committee on Production Guidelines for Book Longevity of the
Council on Library Resources.

Printed in the United States of America

03 02 01 00 99 P 5 4 3 2 1

Library of Congress Cataloging in Publication Data

Chilson, Peter.
   Riding the demon : on the road in West Africa /
Peter Chilson.
      p.   cm.
   Includes bibliographical references and index (p.   ).
   ISBN 0-8203-2036-6 (pbk. : alk. paper)
      1. Niger—Description and travel. 2. Africa, West—Description and
travel. 3. Chilson, Peter—Journeys—Niger. 4. Chilson, Peter—Journeys—
Africa, West. 5. Automobile travel—Niger. 6. Automobile travel—Africa,
West. I. Title.
DT547.27.C47   1998
916.604'329—dc21   98-23609

British Library Cataloging in Publication Data available

For Laura

Contents

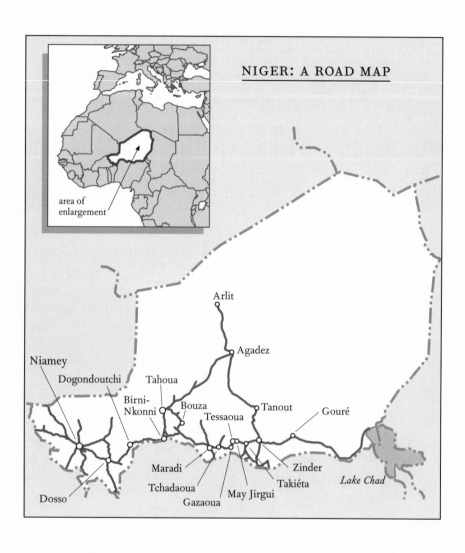

NIGER: A ROAD MAP

area of
enlargement

Arlit

Agadez

Niamey

Dogondoutchi   Tahoua

Birni-   Bouza
Nkonni   Tessaoua   Tanout   Gouré

Maradi   Zinder

Tchadaoua   Takiéta

Dosso   Gazaoua   May Jirgui   Lake Chad

Preface

This is a personal story about road culture, not a work of anthropology. Although I have tried to be fair and accurate on anthropological and historical matters, I may have made generalizations offensive to scholars.

In September 1992 I went to West Africa to gather material for a book. Niger, where I was a Peace Corps volunteer from 1985 to 1987, seemed a logical base for my work. I stayed there a year. An important change has since occurred: In January 1996, Niger's military overthrew the only democratically elected civilian government the country has ever had. Niger's people now live under strict martial law. Arbitrary arrests and police beatings, already widespread before the coup, have grown worse.

But the world of my narrative, the road culture, remains constant. The road has reflected Niger's struggle for survival since the first automobile arrived there at the turn of the century, and it remains a useful metaphor for Africa's fight for stability and prosperity.

The reader will find the following information helpful: Niger, a former French colony, is landlocked and shares borders with seven nations—Burkina Faso to the west, Mali to the northwest, Algeria and Libya to the north, Chad to the east, and Benin and Nigeria to the south. All but Libya and Nigeria are former French colonies, Libya having once been an Italian possession, and Nigeria formerly an English colony.

Moreover, Niger must not be confused with Nigeria, its huge and more complex southern neighbor. Geographically, the countries share a nine-hundred-mile border determined by the colonial powers. They also share the Niger River, which crosses almost three hundred miles of western Niger and continues along Benin's northern border and then south across western Nigeria before emptying into the Atlantic at the Gulf of Guinea.

In 1900 France occupied what it called the "Niger Military Zone" to block British northward expansion. The zone became a colony a few years later. France granted Niger independence in 1960, while preserving military and economic ties.

French, Niger's official language, is the language of education and the civil service and also a neutral communication bridge between Niger's eight distinct ethnic groups and languages. My conversations with the driver Issoufou Garba, my main informant in Niger, were mostly in French, and I relied on French to communicate during most of my travels. I have translated, where necessary, to reflect the best sense of a statement, not necessarily its literal meaning. In passages where I use Hausa, one of Niger's and West Africa's principal languages, the same rule applies.

To avoid confusion in references to people from Niger and Nigeria, I must clarify a difference in spelling: The word *Nigerien* refers to a citizen of Niger, while people of Nigeria are *Nigerians*, the difference being the spelling with *e*, and *a*, respectively.

Finally, a word about currency calculations in the narrative. Like many former French West African colonies, Niger uses the CFA franc, whose value France guarantees. Given daily dollar and CFA franc fluctuations, one dollar generally equaled three hundred francs during my stay.

Acknowledgments

Many people, for all kinds of reasons, own pieces of this book and took risks to help me write it. *Riding the Demon* would not have happened without the guidance and friendship of Issoufou Garba, who always stayed cool, and the help of the late Abdoulaye Mamani, patriot, poet, and teacher.

Hajia Mariatou Moustapha, Niger's only woman commercial driver, let me travel with her. She redefined for me the words *courage* and *integrity*.

I am deeply grateful to my friends Robert Heuer and Henry Marchand, who read the manuscript and gave me the harsh, honest feedback I needed, and their unfailing support. Moreover, during my travels, my family answered my mail, kept the bill collectors at bay, and humored me through rough times.

I am indebted to Toby Thompson, Lesley Hazleton, Peter Schneemann, and John Balaban for supporting this project early on while I was a student in the Master of Fine Arts program in English at Pennsylvania State University. Without their confidence I could not have begun this project.

Special thanks to Paul West, a great teacher and novelist, whose imagination, irreverence, and love of language inspired me.

Thanks to Tom Hale, professor of comparative literature at Penn State, for his sharp insights into African life and for helping me get back to Niger.

Thanks also to the J. William Fulbright Foundation for making possible my travels for this book.

Niger is a very hard place to live and work. Fiona McLaughlin and her husband, Leo Villalon, gave me shelter, food, and, most of all, friendship. I am thankful also to Sue Rosenfeld, a true connoisseur of Niger and West Africa, for her faith in my project and her singular sense of humor.

The staff at Niger's National Archives patiently answered my questions, opened their files, and gave me a place to work even after my research authorization expired. I am grateful as well to the United States Peace Corps for allowing me an occasional place to stay in Niamey, and to the many volunteers who opened their homes to me across Niger.

In Seattle, a writing group provided invaluable support. Thanks to Adrienne Ross, Sue Hacking, and Betsy Geller for their close reading of my work.

Larry Galloway and Sylvia Mantilla at Green River Community College in Auburn, Washington, and Floyd McKay at Western Washington University in Bellingham, gave me enough teaching work to support me while I finished this book.

I am especially grateful to Robley Wilson at the *North American Review* for his steady encouragement of my work and his faith that this story would make a book.

Finally, parts of *Riding the Demon* have appeared in different form in *Ascent, Creative Nonfiction, Exquisite Corpse, Grand Tour,* the *Rain City Review,* and the *North American Review.*

Riding the Demon

> The road is patient, but it does not forgive.
> — Wole Soyinka

The Fickle God

In northern Nigeria, I saw a Peugeot station wagon and a petrol tanker immersed in fire and smoke. The tanker lay on its side, hidden behind gushing clouds of bright orange and black—a gasoline fire. Clouds as big as Volkswagens shot up in dense stacks while the fire expanded into the fields of corn and millet on both sides of the road like slowly spreading wings.

I remember the sound of fire and smoke whispering under a barely audible, stuttering thunder, as if a distant storm were passing. The scene shocked the eyes but soothed the ears. I could not immediately see the demolished Peugeot for the inferno. And I recall realizing that I too had just been riding in a Peugeot station wagon, a bush taxi headed north to the city of Kaduna, where I would get a car to Niger.

I stood on the road beside our car, twenty yards from the fire, and watched as orange flashes at the base of the wreck mushroomed and dissolved in smoke that pushed almost straight up hundreds of feet, where stronger winds carried it south. I could feel the fire's pulse, a hot and warm probing in the breezeless air. Settling ash from the burning fields turned my white T-shirt splotchy gray and smeared my face, neck, and arms. Even without the heat from the fire, the temperature must have been near one hundred degrees. People milled about, dozens at first, and later hundreds, all road travelers.

A man told me the accident had happened twenty minutes earlier. No survivors. The tanker crashed in the pocket of a long curve—made blind by high, thorny prosopis bushes hugging the shoulder—into a bush taxi crowded with people. The impact had turned the Peugeot to paste and scattered it in pieces. A few yards away, a tan chunk of car door lay in a ditch with its window frame intact; nearby, a lump of bloody clothing. A lot more of this sort of thing lay around, more than enough for me. Most of the bodies, the man said, were on the other side of the wreck.

I started to back away and bumped into a small boy, a passenger from another car. Transfixed by the fire, he did not look at me but instinctively clutched at my trousers, standing behind me as if for protection. I was dimly aware of other people, and later realized that very few were watching the wreck as I was. A woman picked up the boy and carried him off the road. More vehicles pulled up, forming a long line. With my eyes on the wreckage, I retreated with slow backward steps, captivated by the feeling that I was witnessing something alive and horrible. A demon feast.

Then I turned away, numbed, and headed for the shade of a tree to try and collect myself. Sitting down, I drew my knees against my chest and put my face against them, hands clasped tightly behind my head, trying to blot out sight and sound. Trying to think.

It was late morning of a day in March 1993. I had been on the road since October. Before dawn, in the city of Ibadan, southern Nigeria, I had bought the last available seat in a white Peugeot station wagon, the four-cylinder model known as a 504. It was a bush taxi, one of the patchwork secondhand cars that define West Africa's public transport. This one carried nine passengers: two men in front with the driver, four men across the middle row (where I sat), and three women in the rear, a cramped space even with two people. The car had no intact windows except for the windshield, and the door on the middle-row right "window" seat, my place, was gone. For hundreds of miles I sat braced against the open air, without a seat belt to restrain me, my left arm thrown across the seat's shoulder so I could grasp the top, my right hand tightly holding the seat in front of me. I had to guess at the driver's speed—always very high—because none of the dashboard gauges worked. And the engine hood would not close. The driver had looped rope through the under latch and tied the hood down to the front fender.

A bush taxi.

Vehicles just like it had filled the Ibadan motor park that morning—bush taxis with no windows, no hoods, no shocks; with balding tires and brakes that whined and screeched. So I took my chances with this one. We left at 6:30 A.M. on the 240-mile trip north to Kaduna. All day the car flew along Nigeria's narrow, crowded arterial north-south highway at speeds around a hundred miles per hour. We sat together, passengers and driver, grim-faced and silent, not uttering a word to one another. Occasionally I heard a soft exclamation, "*Allah!*" or a gasp. Much of the time I kept my eyes closed to protect them from the wind blasting through the door space—and because of the driving. We played chicken on blind curves in the inside lane, passing five, six cars at a time, and always seemed to regain our own lane with only a few feet to spare before we would have smashed into the oncoming traffic.

Regardless of nationality, everyone who drives in Africa drives like this—with heat-inspired, desperate, pedal-to-the-floor insanity, heedless of reason, of their own or anyone else's desire to live beyond the next turn. The driver becomes his vehicle, soaking up the power—enjoying it mentally and physically—lusting for the freedom of unregulated roads. Speed limits are not enforced. He drives as if life must be chased mercilessly to its end and finished in a bright flash.

Our driver that morning stood about six feet five, two hundred muscular pounds of bulk with large, pudgy hands that seemed to grasp the whole top of the steering wheel. He worked in a clean, well-pressed, navy blue wide-collared cotton tunic and matching trousers. A red fez covered his bald head. He handled the car with impatient bravado, the way a teenager might operate a pinball machine, slamming the thing from gear to gear, grumbling and laughing, making turns with wild jerks. With the palm of his right hand he thumped a staccato protest on the top of the dashboard when traffic frustrated him. That habit made it all the more difficult for me to endure this driver, whom I felt certain had lost his mind.

Or maybe I was losing mine to paranoia. Not far south of Kaduna we witnessed, from miles away, the sudden rising of a plume of black smoke. The sight alarmed us instantly. Against a hazy sky, the smoke formed a sharp silhouette over tired, sandy terrain, the West African Sahel, where lingering savanna struggles against invading desert. I had seen many such sights across West Africa, smoke from burning tires and garbage, from farmers clearing fields to prepare for a new crop. Yet this smoke, so dark and ascending so quickly, unnerved me. I thought of the road demons my driver friends in Niger had described to me, beings that appeared on the road suddenly, often in black and in virtually any form, to distract and frighten drivers—to kill them, in fact, and all those with them. An old woman in dark rags, a black bull, a goat, a dog, the silhouette of a horse and its rider, a leviathan black truck covering the whole road and bearing down from the opposite direction. My friends drove with talismans they called *gris-gris* hung from rear and side-view mirrors and steering wheel. Some wore them as necklaces beneath their shirts, like our driver on this trip, a Hausa from northern Nigeria near the border with Niger. His two leather *gris-gris* hung on a cord just below his neck. All of this recalls Nigerian writer Ben Okri's words in his novel *The Famished Road:* "The road swallows people and sometimes at night you can hear them calling for help, begging to be freed from inside its stomach."[1]

Now, under a tree, I sat hugging my knees, feeling that I had been left without an escape route. I thought of fate—the fact that the tanker and Peugeot had collided not long before we arrived on the scene. Fear changes things, stirs up mind and body. I tried to focus on mundane subjects but failed. I could not recall what I'd had for breakfast that morning or what clothes I had worn the day before. I was left suddenly with only bits of myself—a fleeting tangle of thoughts: family, friends, failures, ambitions—as if I were paper shredding in a whirlwind. My abdomen ached, my temples felt numb, my scalp hurt.

I was not involved, knew none of the dead, but fear held me anyway. For months I'd been traveling on roads dominated by predatory soldiers and lined by wrecks, some still burning when I passed. The day before, I had seen a tiny hamlet in southern Nigeria—just four or five mud homes—hours after a single careening eighteen-wheeler had razed it, every house.

There were roads in Niger that suddenly vanished into walls of blowing sand, like a soda straw dunked into chocolate milk. I met and traveled with drivers there who paid homage to the unseen beings controlling the roads. They spent huge sums on protective talismans and sacrifices and then drove with homemade petrol tanks— plastic jugs—sitting in the lap of a passenger, me. I heard people talk of demons of the road, and of the road itself as a fickle god, a compassionate, jealous, violent, hungry being.

In Nigeria, I heard and read of Ogun, the vengeful Yoruba god of iron and the road. One day a Nigerian newspaper headline caught my eye: "Seven Pregnant Women Roasted to Death." The report of the auto accident beneath the headline began with these words: "Thursday January 21, 1993 will always be remembered as a day Ogun decided to feast on the Ukwa Kin Highway."[2]

Months earlier, in Niger, I had bought my own *gris-gris:* three eyeball-sized goatskin pouches filled, perhaps, with Koranic prayers written in Arabic on bits of paper. I could only guess their contents from things I had heard. Issoufou Garba, a driver I came to know well in Niger, told me that *gris-gris* are also filled with grains of blessed soil. Mine were sewn shut and given me by a marabout, a teacher and holy man of Islam, who forbade me to open them so as to protect their sacred value. He told me to keep the *gris-gris* separated from one another in pockets of my pants or my bag. "Be careful," he added, "not to put money in with them."

In my time in Niger I cultivated a sort of road neurosis, beginning with the *gris-gris.* Even when paying for passage in a bush taxi, I argued passionately and bribed shamelessly for the same spot, which I had convinced myself was lucky—the right window seat in the middle row. I don't know why exactly, but that particular seat felt right, far enough away from the front to keep my legs from being pinned and cut off in a head-on collision; and maybe sitting next to the window helped my claustrophobia. I inspected brakes, steering, and tires, pushing drivers and mechanics to exasperation; and I always insisted on seeing the papers of the car and driver, believing this would somehow ensure my safety. Drivers would stare at me in puzzlement, as if I had attacked their integrity, which I had. They would ask, "Don't you trust us?" Other people, even passengers, would laugh at me and say, "He is afraid of death." My neurotic rituals never erased my fears, but they helped control the anguish of travel.

I had to talk myself through every trip with every driver, dozens of journeys, long and short, all the time building a case that traveling in a bush taxi and challenging the odds against dying in a high-speed crash worked to my story's favor. On the road, I scribbled notes—bits of dialogue, landscape details, or lines like, "crazy bastard's going to kill us"—as if the display of hard work would prove the importance of my task to a higher authority, and thus somehow excuse me from death or maiming. A kind of draft deferment owing to my indispensable journalistic existence.

That morning, as we hurtled toward Kaduna and the billowing smoke, my mind was fragmenting. I was thinking I did not know the Nigerian driver's name and did not want to know it. Then, on impulse, I took out my notebook and wrote, "See big plume black smoke not far off. I don't like this."

The road in Africa is more than a direction, a path to take. After you've paid the passage and taken your seat, the road becomes the very concern, the center of life over every mile, a place where you realize, suddenly, that you have surrendered everything. Even the right to survive. The first time on the road in a bush taxi is like boarding a rickety plane or bus only to find you've been kidnapped, which places every experience that follows in a different, sobering light. For me, the term *bush taxi* became far more than just a road transport term; it became an image of memory and road culture.

My first memory is of a road. I was five years old, confused and sad, leaning against a lamppost. I had just watched my father drive off in a blue sedan on another business trip. Details of that morning surface easily: the pimply surface of the silvery steel post against my arm, and the summer heat of 1966, wet and insistent. I recall no other cars, no homes or lawns or bushes. The road governs the memory, as if the world ended right there, on asphalt. Empty, sparkling road. Under the sun, needles of light boiled so the gray surface appeared to move with slight motions of my head, like something on a giant rotating spit, vaguely subversive. A tease. It was only a suburban road in Detroit, but to me it was a gangplank off the fine edge of the universe.

I imagined that all the fighting in green jungles on the TV news happened somewhere nearby that the road touched. My father, I believed, often drove by those terrible things, or through them, never frightened, always knowing what to do. He had been a soldier. Sometimes I would go to the basement closet where his uniform lay in a long cardboard box and sit and look at it, try on the peaked cap, finger the brass buttons on the jacket. These things interested me because they had been down that road, which I wanted to travel, not alone, but in my father's company.

The next summer brought burning and rioting in Detroit, although I didn't understand what it was or where it was happening. Electronic images of violence lunged at us nightly in our living room, all coming, I thought, from the same place: somewhere the road would take me, beyond home and school, like a kidnapper, unless I fought it—which, in the end, I did not. I embraced it.

In the salad of my memory there are bits and pieces about the heart attack that nearly killed my father when I was seven—a scene in a crowded hospital waiting room where a row of empty steel blue wheelchairs waited by a glass door. The heart attack forced a family decision that took us, two years later, from city troubles to a calmer life in the Rocky Mountains. That was twenty-eight years ago.

My father, mother, and two older brothers drove to Colorado. Our belongings went by moving van. I flew with my two younger sisters, staying with relatives en route, escaping the road. I hadn't wanted to escape it, and for years I dreamed about that missed opportunity. I wanted to know, for example, what it was like to approach the Rockies from the Great Plains. I wanted to understand states and borders and distances, to become entangled in the veined terrain of maps, where interstate highways are thick and green, state roads wobble around in red, and lesser roads weave along in various shades and widths of black—all depending on the map, of course.

Around our new home I hiked trails and found abandoned dirt roads that led to old mines—roads that waved, buckled, and snapped. These roads turned driving into a boxing match and required vehicles new to me: all-wheel-drive cars with big tires, extra horsepower, and heavy shocks for terrain that casually busted axles and blew radiators. I loved that excitement. My father's Nissan Patrol broke an axle when one of its front tires plunged through ice into a deep pothole on a mountain road. At seventeen, in the same Nissan on a December evening, I spun out on an icy curve on a dirt road near our home. I remember sitting in the car in a snowy field wondering how I got there. I put it in reverse and bounced right back on the road. Two years later, on another wintry route, I took my eyes off the road for a moment and ended up nose first—but uninjured— in a ditch. My fault, both incidents, but each time it felt like the car had been snatched off the road. Ten years after we moved to Colorado, I went to college and a heart attack killed my father. I have never returned home. Home was Aspen, a resort where wealth distorts reality.

I grew up curious about life elsewhere and consumed books that offered contrast. In sixth grade I discovered Graham Greene and his Liberia memoir, *Journey without Maps*. I liked Greene's sensuous detail and eye for seediness, as in his novel *The Power and the Glory*, in which a man lay on a cot, watching beetles as they "detonated on the ceiling."[3] But I especially liked *Maps*—for its irony and because the book explores expectations of place and self that go awry. I underlined this passage on page 1: "It wasn't the sort of beginning I'd expected when I was accumulating the tent I never used, the hypodermic syringe I left behind, the automatic pistol which remained hidden underneath boots and shoes."[4]

After college, in 1985, I went to West Africa, where I was first a Peace Corps English teacher in Niger and then a journalist based in Ivory Coast. I traveled in bush taxis across a dozen countries. The endurance and ingenuity of drivers, mechanics, and passengers— and their curiously fatalistic view of life—frightened and fascinated me. I first rode a bush taxi on my way to my Peace Corps post. The vehicle, so heavily dented that it resembled a crumpled shoebox, was an early Mercedes heavy truck with a cab that looked out over a wide snout. The radiator hung at an angle, as if someone had tacked it to the front of the engine as an afterthought. I could see steel webbing on the tires where the treads had worn away. Someone had refashioned the trailer by cutting window squares in the sides and installing plywood benches for thirty people. But in fact, some fifty passengers sat inside, squeezed onto bench boards that were screwed into metal frames bolted to the floor. Four men were stacking luggage five feet high on the roof—nylon bags, bed frames, mattresses, grain sacks, a bookcase, bundles of sugarcane, chickens in a palm-rope cage. When I paid my fare, the ticket seller at a wooden table must have read something in my face. He smiled and pointed at the bus. "*Taxi de brousse*," he said—It's a bush taxi.

Inside, I sat on a bench with room for five but packed with nine: two old farmers in tattered khaki robes; three delightfully happy, very large women wearing colorful cotton cloth wraps and carrying a baby each; and me, struggling for a space on the aisle. Cultures blended in this vehicle: Fulani men with fine-boned faces and conical hats; women traveling on market business—women I had seen firmly directing the men loading their goods on the roof; Tuareg men in indigo turbans that hid their faces; and Hausa merchants in bright, wide-flowing robes called *boubous* and striped cylindrical caps. I lost track.

After three and a half years, I left West Africa, exhausted, my nerves raw. I was glad for the respite but dissatisfied with my understanding of the place and its effect on me. That alone does not explain why I wanted to go back and once again face fear on the road. There was as well my curiosity about the road culture and the story it had to tell. And there was restlessness: a desire to know better the outposts of my limitations.

In 1990, I began planning my return to Africa. I spent two years working on my French and Hausa, and studying African transport, history, literature, and religion. I pored over maps and interviewed road engineers and historians. I drew up a research proposal and won a Fulbright grant. I gave up my apartment. I made out my will.

In 1992, I landed back in Niger having decided not to travel the entire continent—too difficult to do without inexhaustible time and money. I chose a tighter focus: to filter the road's story and character through the experience of Niger, the African country I know best. Although my story is chronological, it does not follow a steady geographic progression. I made the southeastern city of Zinder my home base, and I traveled many roads over and over again with the same driver, Issoufou Garba. I wanted to get to know one driver well enough to understand his point of view. I detoured occasionally into Nigeria—whose northern regions share much with Niger culturally and geographically—and hitchhiked from Niamey to Abidjan in Ivory Coast, riding in cotton trucks. In Niger, I also traveled with other bush taxi drivers, truckers, road engineers, an anthropologist, Niger's only licensed woman commercial driver, and a customs officer. In my time on the road I sometimes thought of a Sierra Leonian official who years before told me his opinion of Washington, D.C., which he had visited once. "It makes me crazy," he said. "Those damned traffic lights and speed limits."

It isn't that automobiles or the road hold more cultural importance in Africa than in the West, or that accidents there are more gruesome. Somehow the road takes a more dangerous, visceral, and spiritual position in everyday life in Africa. Demons dwell in wrecks strewn about like the carnage of a vainglorious hunt: a mini-bus upended against a tree as if attempting escape, a blackened truck overturned in a ditch.

Accidents on United States roads attract stares, slow traffic, and are quickly cleared away. On African roads, car wrecks are as common as mile markers. And the remains stay in place for months or years. The violence predates the automobile, tracing its roots to the old Saharan camel caravans that fell under attack by desert nomads, the Tuaregs, and to the destructive itineraries followed by European military missions at the end of the nineteenth century. Those expeditions' pathways often roughly match the motor highways—unintentional monuments to murder and plunder.

The African road is about blood and fear, about the ecstasy of arrival: the relief of finding yourself alive at the end of a journey and the lesser relief of passing unscathed through another army checkpoint. The road is boredom, joy, and terror punctuated by heat in the air and under your feet. The African road is a world of extremes lived out with the punching of a foot against a gas pedal.

As we approached that rising black smoke, I saw a clearer shape: a thick, leaning column like a giant tether to the sky. The driver kept an eye on the smoke and uttered a prayer to himself in Arabic, not his language or mine, but it was a prayer I had heard before and understood: "*Belsfemallah Arahman Arahim*"—a plea for God's protection. Then he struck his chest lightly with his right fist and fell quiet. A moment later, as the plume of smoke got closer, higher, blacker, he mumbled and frowned, shook the index finger of his right hand at the smoke as if he had just identified a thing he'd rather not encounter, and made a sound: "*Yai, yai, yai.*"

The next minute we rounded a curve to see five cars backed up behind flames and smoke on the road, as if the asphalt demon itself had reared up to reveal its face. We were just in time to see a burst of flame as part of the petrol load ignited. The sight sickened me, already fatigued by fear. I could feel myself going up in the flames, wishing it would just happen, finally conclude in a spectacular, painless explosion that would turn my life to vapor and end the fear and uncertainty of the road. When I began traveling, I had not expected this risk, this emotion.

As I sat in the shade of that tree, risk consumed my thoughts. I was nauseous, in need of a walk to clear my head but afraid of what I might find lying on the ground: human remains that might have been mine had I left earlier that morning, reminders of the terrible fate that might lay ahead for me. I didn't think to just walk away from the wreck. Clear thought didn't come. All I knew was on that spot of earth, off the road, I felt safe.

Transport in Africa is a free-for-all system so chaotic that few travelers, even Africans, agree on a precise definition of the bush taxi. Consider this broad interpretation: Bush taxis are dangerous, dilapidated, slow, crowded, demoralizing, and suffocating; they are also fast, intimate, exciting, equalizing, and enlightening. They are bowls of human soup, microscope slides of society, mobile windows on the raw cultural, economic, and political vitality of Africa. Most bush taxis are Peugeot or Toyota station wagons, minibuses, or pickups, but big semis and cars of other makes do the job as well: Renaults, Mercedes, Mitsubishis, Hondas. More specifically, bush taxis are private cars rented out to transport goods and people. They are unregulated; they leave when they are full and arrive whenever. Bush taxis are cheap, are used by all levels of society, and are an important means of transporting trade goods. Any automobile can qualify, but most come secondhand from Europe.

Few Africans own cars, and African governments cannot support large transport systems. Bush taxis fill the void, making up most of the rural motor traffic. Much of what is manufactured, smuggled, or grown in Africa passes weekly through vast, seething outdoor car depots—the motor parks—in cities, and through smaller parks in villages. Similar systems exist in many countries where private car owners are comparatively few, from the Middle East to Southeast Asia, from Africa to South America. In other words, those who own cars cash in on them.

I spoke about bush taxis with John Riverson, a civil engineer from Ghana who studies African rural transport for the World Bank, in Washington, D.C. Riverson views bush taxis as tools of reality. We talked in his cramped office amid shelves of technical reports and photos of road projects.

"There is such a deprivation of transport that people are grateful to have anything that moves," he told me, pointing out that in rural areas most vehicles, government owned or private, serve as bush taxis at some point. Riverson's words called to mind a government ambulance driver in Niger who took on passengers at four dollars a head while delivering medicine to villages in a Land Rover ambulance. Riverson acknowledged the difficulty of defining the bush taxi, but offered this rough guideline: "If we're looking at bush taxis as something identifiable, we're looking at vehicles in the range of three tons' weight"—starting with heavier minibuses, then pickups, station wagons, and sedans. But the number and kinds of vehicles used as bush taxis fluctuate between countries.

Our conversation came down to this: bush taxis are the legacy of an overburdened but vital freelance rural transport network that supports West Africa's economies—a network starved of motor vehicles, spare parts, fuel, mechanics, drivers, and decent roads. Whatever rolls, works.

It occurred to me that the growing crowd on both sides of the wreck was remarkably calm. I hadn't noticed where my fellow passengers had gone, but I realized that only I seemed to be alone. All around me people sat in the shade, sleeping, talking, or eating. Children played and traveling merchants laid out their products on the ground or on small folding wooden tables—clothes, vegetables, cheap jewelry. The scene looked as if all these people, perhaps two hundred by now, were traveling together in one big group. Only small clusters of drivers and a few children paid the burning wreck close attention. This was not a festive crowd, but rather a respectful and patient one that seemed to know better than to argue or complain about something they could not control. Being held up on the road by a calamity was a common event, something not to obsess about but to deal with. Why not sleep or do a little business during the wait?

A man sitting with a woman and a baby a few yards away from me rose to his feet and approached, carrying something wrapped in newspaper. I looked up and smiled, though we had never met.

"Have you got food?" he asked.

"No, I'm not hungry, thank you."

"You will be hungry. You must eat. God knows how long we will be here." He watched me for a moment and then handed me the object in the newspaper. "It's meat, take it."

I was embarrassed but grateful, and I knew better than to refuse a food offering. I shook his hand and took the meat, which turned out to be roasted chicken breast. "Thank you, sir."

"It's nothing, my friend." The man walked back to his family.

In Africa, there are fewer than twenty million motor vehicles to serve 700 million people. The number of cars that actually work is far less. Car accidents in Africa, according to the World Bank, number eight to ten times higher, proportionately, than in developed nations and are a leading cause of death. In Nigeria, home to 90 million people, road accidents consume 2 percent of the gross national product in destroyed vehicles, material, and lives—around 100,000 people injured and ten thousand deaths a year, according to Nigeria's Federal

Road Safety Commission. In contrast, in the United States, with its 250 million people and 145 million passenger cars, the figure hovers around forty thousand deaths each year.

Niger has sixteen thousand passenger vehicles and eighteen thousand commercial cars to serve its 9 million people. There are eight thousand miles of roads, two thousand miles of them paved; the rest are packed dirt road and sandy track. Almost 2,000 people are reported injured annually in road accidents; some 300 of them die. Many, many more injuries and deaths go unreported. Niger's national highway, Route Nationale 1, absorbs half the carnage on its thousand-mile east-west odyssey from Mali to Chad.[5]

Bad driving, poor road and vehicle maintenance, and chaotic traffic are the primary factors to blame for Africa's road deaths, according to a 1990 World Bank study entitled "Transport Policy Issues in Sub-Saharan Africa." The language of this paper employs the wordy bureaucratese of international development documents: "The deterioration of the road networks is causing heavy losses to both the road system itself and to its users and requires urgent action."[6]

On lawless roads the problem is obvious. The human impulse to speed, the desire to get there quickly, takes over. And the bush taxi, more than any other form of transport, rules West Africa's roads.

I have come to know many bush taxi drivers, to like them and sympathize with how they work and live, if not to completely understand their point of view. They see themselves as transporters, honest professionals, survivors forced by circumstances to use guerrilla methods. So, during my travels, I was careful not to express my fears and concerns too bluntly; the drivers do not appreciate hearing about their roguish image. "People think we are irresponsible or thieves," my driver friend Issoufou Garba from Niger once told me. "But they don't understand the difficulty of our work."

In the 1980s, bush taxi drivers struck me as a dashing, reckless male elite, akin to the image of early airplane pilots. The drivers worked blindly and intuitively, vulnerable to technology and the will of a hostile environment: sun, wind, sand, demons, darkness, and checkpoint soldiers. Today, the African bush taxi driver still strikes me as a rogue folk hero: adventurous, kind, cruel, and selfless all at once. A bit like the contradictions inherent in the American cowboy myth—the free-spirited, big-hearted soul with a malicious edge. The drivers, too, are struggling to survive.

It was probably half an hour later, though I'm unsure of the passage of time that day. The tanker was still burning fiercely. No police or emergency services had arrived, and they would not before I left that day. I sat and watched without really seeing. *Can I walk to Kaduna?* I asked myself. *Fifty miles. Three days and I'll be there, still alive. I'll just follow the road and sleep in villages.*

The heat made me think again. In March, even the night offers little temperature relief.

My gaze fell on our driver. When we arrived at the accident, he had huddled with other drivers in discussion. But now he was standing alone, as close to the tanker—perhaps fifteen yards away—as the heat would allow. He stood with folded arms and feet planted a little apart. I'm not sure how long he had been standing there, studying the burning wreck. He stood for fifteen minutes more, moving only to shift his weight from one leg to the other. After a while, I realized what he was thinking, and it scared me. I had seen him scouting detour possibilities just after we arrived at the wreck, but the bush was too thick to drive through. Now, I understood that he wanted to challenge the gods.

He turned around, arms swinging with determination, and strode back to the car. This was both a game and a performance to this man, a career opportunity. He understood other drivers were observing him, waiting to see what he would do.

He opened the door and leaned against the roof, looking first at the fire and then around at his audience. He pursed his lips, raised his shoulders and hands, palms skyward, as if he were asking God for help.

He got into the car, moved it onto the road, and backed up a hundred yards or so. And then we heard him yell: "EEEOOOHHWW!" The wheels of the car spit dirt. He shot forward, aiming for the left side of the wreck, which was pulsing with just as much smoke and fire as when we first arrived. He had seen what others had not: that the haze masked a gap between the rear of the wreck and the bush about the width of his Peugeot.

Issoufou Garba, I thought, would never have risked this—a point to his credit. But I found myself glad this driver had tried. I badly wanted to be gone from this scene, and this man was obliging me.

The taxi disappeared into the smoke and reappeared seconds later on the other side of the wreck where the road began a low ascent. It lifted gently out of the curve where the wreck lay and then stopped.

No one cheered when the driver stepped out from behind the wheel and looked around for his passengers. Time was wasting. Nor did he seem to encourage cheering. Maybe he didn't want to taunt the gods any further. He leaned against the roof, braced by the outstretched palm of his left hand. All at once, drivers and passengers scrambled for vehicles, sprinting to make the run themselves. Hundreds of cars, trucks, and buses lined up on both sides of the wreck to take advantage of that small gap. I thought of an hourglass, but with jumping grains of sand fighting and trampling each other from both sides in their efforts to get through the narrow middle before it closed.

I made my way to the car by going through the bush, around the fire and wreckage. Looking back, I saw a fight start between two drivers, a pushing and shouting match. One man threw a punch to the face of the other, who went down. I heard more shouting in several languages, the rhythmic slap of sandals on cement, engines starting, doors slamming, the soft rumble of flames eating gasoline, and, finally, a siren wailing from the south.

We drove away.

Road Journal

TAKIÉTA, NIGER, NOVEMBER 6, 1992. I'm having nightmares. Cars crashing into each other and people, bodies flying, pieces of bodies all over. Sometimes see soldiers firing, going nuts, screaming for no reason. But never any sound in dreams, never any blood.

Sometimes accidents involve me and I wake up with a gasp, a moan, a shout. I'm riding in a bush taxi and we are about to collide with a truck, but I wake up. Can't catch what it is I shout, if anything intelligible. Had this dream three times now. Each time it gets more violent. The dreams are the clearest I have ever experienced. No doubt frazzled nerves help explain the dreams, but wonder if the malaria pills help cause them.

One can conclude, a little hesitantly perhaps,
that the automobile will kill the camel.
— Maurice Abadie, *La colonie du Niger*

The Dogs of the Road

Niger, by the end of 1992, was a country eager to shed seventeen years of army rule. After a brain tumor felled the dictator. After the army shot and killed nine students in the streets of the capital. After a captain admitted ordering the murder of one hundred Tuareg men, women, and children in the north, and defied government attempts to arrest him. After twenty-five years of drought and the population doubling to nine million. The country wavered on the edge of democracy, flirting with new liberties and new oppressions.

Madness, in brief flashes, framed life. The economy had never been so bad, nor money so scarce. Men built governments and destroyed them. They sat at the steering wheels when buses and bush taxis collided. Men beat men. Men burned cars and buildings. Men decided how women should dress in public and beat and stoned the defiant and negligent ones in the streets. Men set roadblocks, carried arms. At times the country seemed to be at the mercy of male angst, venality, religious fervor. Men framed the limits of sanity and madness. They decided who would ride the roads, and who would not.

October 1992. My journey began early in the morning at Wadata, the central motor park in Niamey, Niger's capital. There, three afternoons a week, road travelers watched an Air Afrique DC-10 leave Niger's nearby international airport to return to Paris. The aircraft announced itself with an incandescent roar, emerging almost immediately above the trees on the edge of the motor park's sandy expanse. The gleaming fuselage, dignified by a green stripe, passed over fleets of buses and cars with the patience of a stray cloud.

Once overhead, the plane appeared to hover, enjoying both the awed stares of the children and adults arriving from and departing for villages and towns and the more resigned looks of the park's regular inhabitants—the drivers, vendors, mechanics, beggars, and thieves. Then, abruptly, as if bored, the DC-10 roared louder, like a rude yawn, and banked sharply north to make its way over the Sahara Desert to North Africa, the Mediterranean Sea, and Paris.

Wadata—a Hausa word that means "place of economic well-being"—is an open market and motor park, a great, sandy lot swarming with thousands of people and hundreds of automobiles, all terribly overloaded and in various states of disrepair. Automobiles careen through the dust, weaving among donkeys and camels. The camels plod gracefully, heads raised in looks of smug concern, while the donkeys mix panic with stubbornness, sounding rusty screeches at a run or standing still in silent indignation.

The African motor park, the fountainhead of the road, is a combination of open bazaar, cattle drive, and drag race. Men and boys hawk piles of cloth, sunglasses, jewelry, candies, cheap perfumes, packaged soaps, and deodorants with names like He Man (in a cardboard box with a military camouflage design) and Money, all piled together in rippling, multicolored, escalating rows atop wooden tables. Little girls sell hard-boiled eggs, peanuts, and vegetables from trays they balance on their heads; women sit on mats in the shade of trees behind mounds of tomatoes and onions. Women dominate the food markets of the large motor parks, but on the road they are passengers, often silent, in the bush taxis and buses. In the chaos of large motor parks, amid odors of cooking meat and vegetables merging with fumes of sweat and excrement and petrol, you see a kind of order in the segregation of the sexes—until you become preoccupied with the heat and the odors assaulting your nose. The smells sting, scraping the inside of your nostrils and making your eyes water until you grow accustomed to it all.

I sat on a bench in dense heat, waiting to buy a ticket for a bus trip the next morning to eastern Niger on Route Nationale 1. A boy a few feet away from me said in French to his comrades: "You watch, one day I will be on that plane." I had no particular destination in mind, except to be somewhere east by nightfall. My idea was to spend a month getting a feel for the country's road system.

Some facts: Niger is a large desert country more than twice the size of France. It has neither railroads nor domestic airlines. Niger's nearly three-hundred-mile fragment of the Niger River crosses its far western edge and is useless to most of the population. Many people travel only by foot. Route 1 runs west to east along the country's southern rim, peppered by some fifty-five military, customs, and police checkpoints along its length.

A few yards away from where I sat, a red, green, and yellow bus rested on its axles. The engine cavity was empty. The bus had once served the route between Niamey and Accra, the Ghanaian seaside capital. Now it listed in the sand like a grounded tugboat, a fading English motto painted across its rear: "Oh, Don't Worry!"

I was worrying—about bad roads, crashes, crazy drivers, and moody soldiers. Automobile travelers in Africa brick over their visual and mental records of the road. Riders submit mutely to intimate discomfort, skin melting in peanut butter heat in vehicles that are rebuilt time and again and driven until they either wreck or fall apart.

At a dinner in Niamey days before, I had told an American diplomat that I wanted to write about the road. He stared at me. "I went out east," he said, "you know, to see the giraffes, and I saw bush taxis broken down on the road—out in the middle of nowhere! Christ, in the bush, when you break down, you're screwed. There's nothing you can do. You're just out there."

When I returned to Wadata in the morning to begin the trip east, I boarded an old Mercedes tour bus with sixty-six seats and decent tires, without intact windows or a hood to cover the engine. At 8:00 A.M. the coach left the city. An apprentice mechanic, a boy of about twelve, crouched like a stowaway in the stairwell below the driver. It was his job to show the vehicle papers at roadblocks, pay bribes, and monitor the engine. The driver called him *karamota*—Hausa for "dog of the car"—but he let the boy do his work.

After two hundred miles, in the early evening near the border with Nigeria, a barefoot man in a sweaty T-shirt and brown trousers leaped on the road from a hiding place in the bush, waving wildly. We slammed to a halt. The driver stepped out and greeted him with a smile, a hand on the shoulder. The man heaved and gasped, bending to rest his hands on his knees. Then he jumped back into the tangled bush, only to scramble up the road embankment a minute later with a black forty-liter plastic jug on his head—black-market fuel from Nigeria. This was a clandestine deal, prearranged. A gasoline stop in Niger.

The smuggler was too thin, with a hollow-cheeked, V-shaped face. Burrs covered his hair, and he had the exhausted, open-mouthed look of a man who had been waiting in prosopis thorns all day without water or food. The boy and driver lifted the load off his head to pour it in the gas tank at the rear of the bus. Again, our man ran into the bush. We all watched him. Then we lost sight of him. There was a frantic thrashing sound, first in one direction, then the other. I caught a glimpse of his head bobbing above vegetation, arms swinging at the bush like a drowning man fighting for air. He had apparently forgotten where he put another jug, but he soon came jogging up the embankment—jogging with a full forty-liter container on his head.

The driver paid four thousand CFA francs (roughly thirteen dollars) for eighty liters, a third less than the legal stuff at government gas stations. The man took the money and vanished into the thorns.

During the thirteen-hour, 240-mile journey, we stopped to put water in the radiator, for an identity check at a checkpoint, to repair a flat tire, to pray, to fix another flat tire, for a baggage search at a checkpoint, to put more water in the radiator, to pray again, to replace a fan belt, to be searched at another checkpoint, and to pray again.

In Madaoua, the town where the bus left me, about forty miles east of our gas stop, I sheltered at a Baptist mission. A missionary couple—an Australian woman and a Canadian man—gave me Earl Grey tea and tried to make sense of me. They seemed convinced that I was on the road to moral oblivion. I talked about marabouts who made amulets for protection on the road, about the petrol smuggler, bush taxis, and colonial road builders.

About 11:00 P.M. they asked me to join hands with them and kneel on the living room floor to pray. "Lord, we ask," they whispered, "that you protect Peter during his journey on the road, that you guide him to eternal light away from the wide road toward Hell and onto the narrow road of salvation in your name." I thanked them and went to bed.

Friendly people. They fed me that night. But the next morning, as I stood in the doorway with my bag, they warned me of "the darkness of Islam" and "the emptiness of animism." I smiled politely as I listened to them, but I walked away in a bad mood. The "wide road" was exactly my destination. I bought passage, with five others, in a Peugeot sedan, a bush taxi, which carried me farther east up Route 1.

Route 1 is six yards wide and as many inches thick. It stretches like the vertebrae of a sturgeon across Niger, from the border with Mali in the northwest, to the desert town of Nguigmi on the dry basin of Lake Chad in the southeast. Most of the way the road flirts with the nine-hundred-mile-long Niger-Nigeria border, almost touching it at times, then veering off, but never far. In places, Route 1 parallels camel caravan routes that for centuries supported trade across the Sahara. The road is a polite presence coated in lumpy gray asphalt. Yet it remains critical to Niger's economic, social, political life.

A megalomaniacal French explorer named Captain Paul Voulet unknowingly plotted Route 1's course in 1899, killing, plundering, and then dying along its path. A village hosts his body in a crumbling, cement-encased grave a few hundred feet from the asphalt. In the road's early years, forced labor crews—men, women, children, the crippled and the healthy—built and maintained Route 1 at the cost of hundreds of lives. For decades it served as a tube through which the region's few natural resources—mostly agricultural— were funneled south to ships bound for Europe from ports like Cotonou and Abidjan. A mangled tinsel of auto wrecks trims the road's shoulders. Its length is patrolled by underpaid, vindictive soldiers. Untrained, disgruntled men make a living driving it. Route 1 crosses some of the world's most arid, hot, and barren land: the northern edge of the Sahel, a territory marooned by drought. It traverses Niger's most populated territory, bisecting ethnic boundaries.

As you stand on the road, your eye scrapes along a landscape where neem, palm, and baobab forests—sacrificed to crops, cooking fires, and desert—disintegrated long ago. In places the soil has surrendered to strong winds. Lions, elephants, giraffes retreated south or were hunted down. Fields of laterite rock and sand now claim much of the plain: a maroon underskin, raw and pockmarked. Thorny prosopis bushes poke through thin cracks.

Route 1's sordid history and official name, la Route de l'Unité, suggest something aggressive and imposing, like Interstate 80, or flamboyant, like a bullet train. Instead, it is a long and lonely stretch, more like a county service road in southern Idaho than a major highway. Route 1 looks sick: narrow, emaciated, heavily pitted in places, and almost totally invisible to someone standing a few feet off in the bush. A road undercover. Chunks of it vanish beneath an uneven film of drifting sand and settling dust.

The German explorer Heinrich Barth, funded by the British Royal Geographic Society, wrote of a storm that engulfed his camel caravan in 1853, near what was then the village of Niamey. He reported "a most fearful sand-wind, which enveloped the whole district in the darkness of night."[1]

Blowing sand camouflages the road, which resembles a fading tattoo on the bright yellow grasses and brown soil of the Sahelien savanna. Low floodplains sometimes obscure this camouflage. In such places, government engineers raise the road embankment and fortify it with stone masonry to stem the assaults of summer monsoon floods.

Bush taxis, buses, and heavy trucks also betray the road's presence with sudden and sometimes brutal appearances, as if they have awakened a monster angry at being unmasked. Horribly overloaded vehicles hurtle down the narrow corridor at frenzied speeds, like fleeing refugees.

Many roads that cross the Sahel are like this: deceptive. They scare no animals, unlike the railroads that terrified buffalo herds on the American Great Plains, dividing millions of animals into separate stampedes. Yet West Africa's major roads do make a reliable record of the colonialism that separated so many peoples. French officers assigned to hunt Captain Voulet's renegade expedition discovered the carnage of the thousands he murdered in villages that now sit on Route 1—corpses of children hanging from trees, tangled bodies clogging wells. "All along the road, tired porters who could not or would not walk further were shot or bayoneted," wrote one investigating officer of Voulet's depredations.[2]

Like a sneak attack, Route 1 behaves as if it appeared only hours ago, mysterious, a seemingly friendly yet poisonous growth, unobtrusive and harmless until you touch it.

Days after parting with the missionaries, I arrived two hundred miles up the road in the village of Takiéta, where another road comes north from Nigeria to join Route 1. A Peace Corps volunteer put me up for three days. Evenings I spent sitting at a roadside tea table, quietly sipping the brew and watching a checkpoint staffed by soldiers in red and green berets. Red for Niger's Garde Republicaine, green for the gendarmes of the Brigade Routière, the highway patrol.

I watched a Toyota minibus packed with travelers and luggage at the checkpoint. The driver was in his twenties—in Niger, the driving profession demands youth—dressed in jeans, T-shirt, sandals. He spent an hour talking with three soldiers, head bowed but looking calm, serious, perhaps risking something by not assuming the tone of sycophancy common at checkpoints. The soldiers laughed, and one slapped him with the open palm of his hand. At this, the driver stopped talking. He stopped bowing his head. For another hour he stood in place, silent and still, glaring at the soldiers. What started as a negotiation became an issue of honor, and of nerves.

The soldiers let him and the minibus go.

In this spot, just a few miles from the Nigerian border, soldiers were collecting money, usually five-hundred-franc "taxes" (roughly $1.70 at the time) on bush taxis and private cars. They took thousands of francs more from smugglers in ancient Ford and Mercedes vans—1950s models that often had no working lights—then waved them through the checkpoints. The vans were packed full and piled high with legitimate goods like scrap metal, lumber, kola nuts, cloth, sugarcane. Some of the drivers stopped at my table for tea. I learned they also carried boxes of contraband American and French cigarettes, barrels of Nigerian gasoline, hashish, marijuana seeds— and, one driver boasted, cartons of automatic weapons bound for Tuareg rebels in the Sahara. A buffet spread of a nation's economy and politics.

Once in a while a crash illuminates the night in the bush, to the pleasure of the gods, when some poor driver hits a lightless vehicle, releasing the demons in the gasoline barrels. Charred remains line the road shoulder for the thirty-two miles from Takiéta east to the old provincial capital and market city of Zinder. Fresh flames of wrecks sometimes startle the dark night on Route 1, flashing bright stains on the air. Villagers comb the wrecks for salvageable spare parts to sell—a hubcap, a fuel filter—the moment the metal cools.

Twelve miles east of Takiéta, in the village of Tirmini, ragged boys besiege bush taxis. They wave plastic funnels with long hoses and shout prices for Nigerian gasoline. They demand more than ask, *"Combien tu veux? Combien tu veux?"* Smugglers dilute gasoline with water, and fuel is often contaminated with sand, bits of paper, and plastic during its journey from Nigerian refineries. But the gas is cheap (forty cents a liter at that time), less than a third the price of the legal stuff sold at British Petroleum and French Elf stations around Niger.

The morning I left Takiéta, I was waiting for the taxi driver to negotiate for fuel when I felt something soft bump against my ankles. I looked down to see a dusty boy in faded red nylon basketball shorts with dead, emaciated limbs, like discarded chicken bones. He smiled at me and, in a hoarse voice, begged for money, *"Cadeau, Monsieur, cadeau, cadeau."* Then he rolled off down Route 1—not on a wooden trolley, but on the ground, through the dirt, his body propelled by the swinging momentum of dead limbs, over and over. I stared after him.

The central motor park in Zinder is an open dirt space that resembles a crude stock exchange. People trade, sometimes furiously, in transport, auto parts, gasoline, currency, and news. The motor park collects people, drifters, beggars, and job seekers, who take up residence and grow in numbers. A mechanic works under a corrugated tin scrap, its corners wired to wooden posts. The tin bends in a shallow U under the weight of banana peels, mango pits, broken parts; it might one day collapse on the mechanic's bare back. Young women in bright cotton wraps and T-shirts weave through the crowds with trays of eggs, peanuts, and mangos atop their heads. Black-market money traders in bright *boubous* of blue and green and orange perch on stools fingering cash spread on cloths in front of them: ankle-high stacks of bills and coins from Niger, Chad, Nigeria.

In the motor park, drivers told me that rumors of a transport strike had been circulating for months. They complained about the bribe demands at checkpoints. Soldiers arbitrarily beat drivers, they told me, and seized vehicles and goods. "We can close this road. The country will be on its knees, and the government will be begging us to open the roads," one driver said. They could close the roads, no doubt. But I wondered whether these men had the resources to keep their families alive during a strike. If a strike started, though, I wanted to be on the road, with the drivers, to see what would happen.

On November 9, I went to the headquarters of the Zinder bureau of the Syndicat National des Conducteurs Nigerien—the drivers' union—in a square office in a cement building beside the motor park. The union represents bush taxi and truck drivers. I found three men chatting in French around a wooden table. I heard one say: "The military, they are all thieves." Then they looked up and saw me standing in the doorway.

"What do you want?" The voice wasn't unfriendly, just surprised. The speaker's clear-lens aviator glasses hung on the edge of his nose, above a smile. He wore an old kaftan over dark trousers and a black watch cap on the very top of his head.

"Are you drivers?" I asked.

The men nodded. "*Oui*," said one.

"I'm traveling. Can you tell me if there will be a strike? Everyone around the motor park seems to be talking about one." My question invited subdued laughter, born, perhaps, of the thought of a foreigner getting caught in their struggle. I tried to smile.

The man in the glasses said, "We can't say. But you know, the only safe place now is Niamey. My advice is to leave now."

"How long do you think the strike will last?"

The men smiled at each other. "Already, you are asking too many questions," said the one in glasses. He did all the talking. "We haven't even said there will be a strike, and who knows how long a strike would last."

I introduced myself and explained, impulsively, that I was a writer interested in road transport in Niger. I hoped this revelation would get me some inside information. The man in the glasses remained silent, looking at me without expression. "The road is a difficult place to work," said one of the other men. "What else is there to know?"

But the man in the glasses seemed more accommodating. "Maybe the road is where you should be right now," he said. I nodded. "We are all drivers here. Come and see us if you return to Zinder. Ask for me. I drive one of the white Peugeots you see outside." Several white Peugeot station wagons were parked on a wide sandy median strip between two one-way streets.

I gave the man my name, written on a piece of paper. He, in turn, wrote down his name and title in French and gave them to me. "Issoufou Garba, driver, member of the drivers' union, Zinder."

I took one of those Peugeots back as far as Madaoua, where I chose to wait at a small hotel. At dawn on November 11, I awoke to the sounds of car horns, shouting, and shattering glass—a car being sacked. The road through town was clogged with a slow parade of cars and trucks, men and boys. There were no women or girls. I joined the procession, which was heading west, out of town. The marchers shouted slogans like, "*Fin a la corruption!*" and "*Justice, Justice!*" We walked past the checkpoint as soldiers looked on. They continued to watch as strikers built a roadblock a few hundred yards down the road. Boys arrived with sticks, pipes, and knives.

During the strike I saw few women and girls, except for some stranded women travelers at the Madaoua motor park and one young woman who came to the roadblock with a covered pot of rice and beans for the union strikers. Along the road, during the strike, it sometimes seemed as if the female population had evaporated.

A union man looking on shook his head. I heard him say, "This is a thieves' strike." I thought to myself that this was a boys' strike.

I learned later that things were worse elsewhere. Prices for everything shot up; hoodlums beat and robbed motorists indiscriminately, burning and stealing their cars. Troops with machine guns guarded motor parks and the offices of the government bus line, but they left the strike barriers alone. Truckers maneuvered their rigs to form ten-mile queues blocking roads to international border posts, while the government refused to acknowledge the crisis.

At first, all over the country, the union men, buttressed by the gangs, blocked major and minor roads with logs, rocks, pieces of wrecked cars—the skeleton of a sedan, discarded wheel axles, the mangled chassis of a pickup—to stop anyone from using *their* roads. In the end, however, only armed boys remained at the barriers; the union men, with their leaflets and proclamations, just drifted away. The soldiers played cards.

At 8:00 A.M. I stood watching at the Madaoua strike barrier, hoping to get a ride west on Route 1. Then things began to happen. In my notebook I recorded this: "A man in a battered white Peugeot pickup truck drove down the road from the town, and would have been firmly turned back but for his excessive speed. He ran a road barrier at its weakest point, plowing through a pile of twisted car fenders and rocks, only to lose control and spin out in a column of dust." The truck balanced for a moment on its left-side wheels before dropping back down on all fours. Boys swarmed over it, yanking open doors, pulling the man from both directions, beating him with feet, chains, clubs. Blood dribbled down his face in thin lines as clubs fell on the windshield, shattering it. The man tumbled unconscious onto the road. The boys tossed him in the back of the truck, and a half dozen of them climbed into the truck bed as one got behind the wheel to take the truck on a victory tour. They whooped and screamed, waving their weapons and holding up the arms of the bloodied man. I never saw them again.

I had landed in chaos. The union drivers and the boy gangs tolerated me. "Yes, yes, write it all down," they said. "It's not for nothing that we do this." In view of the official corruption at checkpoints, it was not difficult for me to understand the anger behind the strike, and to empathize. Once, I felt the impulse to drop my pen, pick up an iron pipe, and engage in a little violence of my own: put the metal through the windshield of a police Land Rover; let it fall on the Mercedes driven by the government official who sold donated food and medicines—goods intended for starving people—on the black market; perhaps even let go one good swing at his head.

I didn't. No guts. No way to cover my tracks.

The drivers' strike had begun at noon, in hundred-degree heat, after a season of rains that only teased, like a promised glass of cool water suddenly denied. The strikers intended noble things: to protest police and military corruption on the roads and force the government to action. Instead, mobs ruled Niger's roads—motor park touts, thieves, apprentice mechanics, street vendors, many under the age of eighteen. Some were barefoot, some wore ragged shorts or cast-off jeans and dirty T-shirts bearing slogans like "Go Penn State!" The union, struggling to bring integrity to the roads, had lost the initiative to angry mobs frustrated by starvation and dictatorship. The strike was meant to cleanse the arteries. Instead, the country began to hemorrhage.

No one was going anywhere very fast.

This I had to see. I bought a warm Coke from a boy carrying a plastic ice chest on his head and leaned against the bridge's steel railing to watch. A Nigerien customs officer dressed in civilian clothes—blue shirt and trousers—was in a jam, a loud and crowded situation with excited, angry young men shaking fists and shouting: "*Brûlez le! Brûlez le!*"—Burn it! Burn it! They meant his shiny black Peugeot 504 sedan—a color reserved by law in Niger exclusively for high officials. He was standing in front of the car on the bridge to the town of Birni-Nkonni, pleading with the strikers. Someone shouted: "We can kill you here."

I watched this from the bridge, having just arrived from Madaoua in the car of an Arab merchant. About 4:00 P.M., I had bribed the boys back in Madaoua with a five-hundred-franc bill to let me ride out in the merchant's Toyota pickup. The Arab had, I assumed, given the boys a lot of money for the right to pass. He also, I found out at the bridge, knew the customs man, Lowali Moumouni. When we arrived the mob had blocked the road, so we stood and watched. My Arab companion pointed to Moumouni and looked with, with relish or concern I couldn't tell. "He's the customs chief of the region," he told me.

Moumouni behaved impressively. He talked calmly, without anger or fear, to people who wanted to put his eyes out. He listened, frowned, even smiled. He was smooth, physically steady, like a man discussing an ordinary purchase, though I couldn't hear his voice. After forty-five minutes the customs man appeared to get his way. The shouting ceased and men drifted off, apparently satisfied. Moumouni was shaking hands and laughing with some men. The mob had decided to let him and a few vehicles pass, my Arab friend included.

Around 10:00 P.M. that evening, I sat on a roadside in Birni-Nkonni, hoping and reading. Along with five other men, I was awaiting the return of a man who ran a market stall. He had said he knew another man willing to drive us to Niamey for five thousand francs apiece, three times the usual price.

I was thinking about transport literature from various development agencies. From my bag I took a World Bank report, a document with a brown-and-white cover bearing the title "Transport Policy Issues in Sub-Saharan Africa." I read by flashlight to lure sleep. "The increasing demands on transport parastatals to provide services below cost, and to fulfill roles unrelated to their main service objectives, are having severe negative consequences on the enterprises' financial situation."[3]

Imprecise and expensive language. Where were the engineers and bureaucrats now? Main service objectives? I dropped the report in the dirt.

A set of headlights approached and slowed to a stop in front of us. From inside the car, a man's voice asked in good French: "Monsieur, where are you going?" I looked up, blinded. "Are you traveling to Niamey?" he asked. I was still unsure whom he was speaking to. "Can I give you a lift?" A door slammed and someone walked around the back of the car and stood in front of me, a silhouette sticking a hand out in greeting. "Are you not the white man I saw on the bridge?" It was Moumouni, the customs officer.

I wanted to leave the report behind, but Moumouni retrieved it while I put my bag in the backseat and politely handed it to me, saying, "*Vous l'avez oublié*"—You forgot it—and walked around to his door. He never acknowledged the other men on the road, who sat up and stared. It occurred to me as we pulled away that Moumouni was every smuggler's and driver's Enemy Number One, that riding with this man on this night was either the very thing needed to get through the gauntlet or a good way to get killed.

Once we were seated in his black Peugeot sedan, Moumouni said to me, "You know, I'm supposed to be on vacation." With a customs officer for my traveling companion, I saw the road hierarchy turned on its head. We flew through checkpoints, slowing only enough to acknowledge the soldiers and give them a chance to see his official plates. Between towns he averaged eighty miles an hour with the windows open and the stereo blaring Bob Marley.

"You like the car?" he asked in French.

"What?"

"I said, do you like my car?" He turned down Bob Marley a bit.

"Oh yes, it's in good shape. Did you buy it in France?"

"*Mon dieu, non!* I bought it off a tourist. A Frenchman drove it across the desert. A 1990 model, three thousand dollars. It was white, you know; I repainted it myself."

"You paid in dollars?"

"Oh, no. I just think in dollars." He grinned at me. Even for a man of his position, three thousand dollars was more than a year's salary.

"I used to have another Peugeot that I bought in Nigeria," he said. "But I rolled it last year, driving at night. I fell asleep." He shrugged. "The car was destroyed, but I was fine."

"Why do you still drive so fast?"

"You haven't seen? There is so much insecurity on the road these days. Speed is necessary. I take no chances. I paid off those men at the bridge, but if things get really difficult, I have this"—he patted a small bulge under his right armpit. A pistol? He didn't say and I didn't ask. Moumouni looked fiftyish, short and chubby with white stubble on his head, but still quick on his feet. The pistol comforted me, but my respect for him dimmed.

We drove a hundred miles to the next strike roadblock in a town called Dogondoutchi. Cars and heavy trucks were backed up more than a mile. Men stood in small groups, talking, smoking, waiting. Moumouni, taking the left lane, drove to the front of the line and parked. I stayed behind while he went "to see someone." He returned a few minutes later with a young man who held the car keys. Moumouni said to me: "You and I will walk."

We did. We crossed the barrier of rocks and logs. We walked past two still smoking wrecks and sleeping men rolled up in sheets on mats beside their vehicles. We walked twenty minutes or so to the end of the line of cars, where we found the Peugeot on the roadside and the young man waiting at the wheel, smoking. He got out and handed Moumouni the keys in exchange for a five-thousand-franc note and walked away. The young man had detoured through the bush, around the roadblock.

"He's a union driver," Moumouni said. "A friend."

Ninety minutes later we arrived at the western exit of the city of Dosso, an hour east of Niamey. We sat in the car studying a roadblock of dozens of union minibuses parked bumper to bumper. The line of vehicles formed a bow across the road and down into the bush on both sides to stop anyone who might want to drive around, like us. In the moonlight, the machines looked like skulls. Parked up and down the road from the barrier were hundreds of trapped vehicles.

Walking, I followed Moumouni off the road and down the line of minibuses. We stepped over dozens of men sleeping on mats or bare ground—drivers wrapped ghoulishly in sheets, apprentices with their heads wound in towels or shirts to protect them against the mosquitoes. Every few seconds we heard the slap of a hand on flesh. In the gray moonlight the scene resembled a massacre, a convoy that had been strafed from the air. No one challenged us as we poked through the bush around the south end of the barrier and discovered a sandy and bumpy track.

"That's it," Moumouni whispered. We traced the track back to where it met the road and then jogged to his car. He put it in reverse and backed the vehicle up past the junction with the track. Some men raised their heads from sleep just to look. We hit the track at a running start, swerving in the sand but continuing for some minutes until we got stuck. As if on cue, two teenage schoolboys in trousers and white collared shirts stepped out of the bush and offered to help— for five hundred francs apiece.

We entered Niamey at 6:00 A.M. on the strike's second day. The sun was rising, and in a few hours the government would open negotiations with the union. The strike would last another four days. And the soldiers would continue taking money.

Somewhere, too, the planes were fighting forward; the
night flights went on and on like a persistent malady.
— Antoine de Saint Exupéry, *Night Flight*

A Driver, a Checkpoint, an African Road

Issoufou Garba was negotiating with a man who had him pinned
back against the driver's door of his car. Issoufou said, "Hassan, are
you going to kiss me?" He added: "I paid you." Issoufou began to laugh,
his shoulders in the grasp of a man who had just withdrawn his hands
from around Issoufou's neck and now leaned over him, demanding
more money. It was a negotiating tactic of the *komasho*—a freelance
bush taxi ticket agent who sells passengers to drivers such as Issoufou.

"I swear, Issoufou, you are becoming a white man, whiter than a
white man," said the *komasho*. "You are George Bush." Hassan pronounced that last name with a sharp burst of air: "Boosshh." The
comment credited my friend's stubbornness, his wealth. Issoufou
could have pushed the man away. Hassan was, after all, thinner,
weaker, dirty. Pathetic.

Like a grassroots travel agent, the *komasho* trades in passengers.
Working in Niger's motor parks, the *komasho* helps drivers find passengers, or he buys them from another *komasho* and then resells them
to drivers. All without consulting the passengers, of course. In the

West African motor park, the passenger is a simple commodity—having secured a place in one car, he often finds himself traded to another, or even abandoned.

Hassan's exhortations brought on a deep, grit-choked cough. He bent over, resting hands on knees. Issoufou didn't move away. He placed his hand on Hassan's back and said, "*Patience petit frère.*" Then he added, "God provides." Hassan, his face and hair whitened by dust, clutched a dirty cotton robe about him against the wind. The coughing spasm faded; he looked up, breathing hard. "*Issouf, s'il te plaît,* I'm asking for something more, in God's name, as a favor for loyal service."

I wanted to end the scene, just walk over and hand Hassan some money to appease him and my conscience, but I did nothing. That was the agreement. My desire was to learn, I'd told Issoufou when we first discussed traveling together. That was fine, he said, "but you will pay for your seat and you will never interfere with my work."

From a breast pocket of his gray tunic, Issoufou pulled a one-hundred-franc piece and gave it to Hassan, slapping it into his open palm with a single, pronounced shake of the *komasho*'s hand. It was a gesture Issoufou wanted him to remember. It meant, "Don't bother me." Hassan pinched the coin between thumb and fingers of both hands, the way a Catholic priest offers the communion host, and cocked his head, as if to say, "Oh, come on!" Issoufou laughed and squeezed Hassan's shoulder.

Issoufou was not a physically remarkable man. He was short and pudgy. Noncorrective aviator glasses balanced crookedly on the end of his nose, giving him a goofy look. He presented to the world an unobtrusive, fleshy face. Yet he also projected casual control, as if nothing mattered. Not time, not money. He had the sort of cool that reins in another man's anger.

Road cool.

The *komasho* pleaded, "*Issouf, au nom de dieu*"—in God's name. But Issoufou turned away and opened the car door, the departure signal for me and seven other passengers: two women and five men. "*Issouf, s'il te plaît.*" Hassan grabbed his elbow. "*Issooouuuf!*"

Issoufou's laugh cut back to a trace of smile. He said: "I have paid you, Hassan. Let me pass."

Unobstructed, Issoufou got in the car and eased the machine forward in first gear, speeding up a bit as we passed through the thick crowd. We covered the last few yards to the motor park gate and police post, a small cement hut where Issoufou began *les formalités:* A policeman in fatigues and black beret waited to check the car registration and travel log, and to collect a five-hundred-franc exit tax before signing the log.

I checked my watch: 7:10 A.M.

Issoufou Garba was both my guide and my friend on the roads of Niger, but I was powerless to aid him during our journeys. We traveled together for seven months in his 1978 Peugeot 504 *familial*. A real road hugger. I stood by during angry negotiations, saw wads of bills in shaking fists, observed the occasional hand at Issoufou's throat. These things preceded access to the road. They had to be taken for granted, endured as routine, the way of business and life in the motor parks and on the road in Niger. Border crossings.

Issoufou liked a bit of distance between us. So I hung back.

He was thirty-seven years old when I met him, soft-spoken, patient, meticulous in business. He was a good client of many *komasho* in many cities, and he understood how to handle them. He rarely showed anger or betrayed fear. And, having seen more than once the force of a *komasho*'s wrath, I respected our agreement. Better to let Issoufou handle things.

Issoufou was as heavy on the gas pedal as any driver, but he also defined the bush taxi driver's struggle with a softer edge. He cut his speed to an average eighty miles an hour when he had women and children in the car. At the wheel, he was relaxed but firm, a two-hands driver not fond of blind curves or compulsive passing. Issoufou did not like games. These things helped me endure the road with him— the wrath of gendarmes, the frustration of breaking down miles from anywhere, the heat and wind, the high speeds, and, for me, the unending fear.

Issoufou was in his fifth year of driving a bush taxi. He owned three. He had been an accountant, a street vendor, a gasoline smuggler, a prisoner. At the time, he was finally making money, but earning it in a line of work with little more job security than a tail gunner would have. Dangerous roads in tough times. Issoufou told me these things easily, eagerly, when I returned to Zinder in early December and looked him up at the drivers' union office. I found him there at 4:00 P.M., sitting at the same table as before, reading a worn copy of a French picture romance magazine.

He rose and shook my hand. "I see you survived the strike. I'm glad you have come back." Encouraged, I sat down and told him my story—about the violence at the roadblocks, about the customs officer and the black Peugeot and the pistol the officer kept under his tunic, but I did not mention the bribes I saw union men take. I didn't want to lose Issoufou's good faith before I even had it. He ignored what I said about the gangs of boys and delighted in the details of the customs man. "Where does he get the money for a new black Peugeot?" Issoufou asked, without needing an answer. He shook his head. "They are all thieves."

"No question of that," I said.

"So, Monsieur Peter," he said, "are you going to stay with us awhile here in Zinder?"

I offered Issoufou my proposal. "You know I'm interested in your work. I want to know more about the life of the bush taxi driver."

He smiled. I continued. "Yes, I'd like to spend some time here, perhaps even ride with you if you don't think I'd be in the way."

To my surprise, Issoufou needed no convincing. He was eager to work with me, though I would often wonder in later months whether he regretted that decision. Issoufou nodded at my shoulder bag. "Get out your notebook," he said. "And let's talk. People need to know what we drivers are about." Our negotiations began there.

Cool air—a blast of the Harmattan wind—scraped my nerves. I tried to spit out the grit that coated the walls of my mouth and nose into air already saturated with it. When I arrived at the Zinder motor park just after dawn, a shroud of fine swirling dust blurred the scene. An old man in brown robes walked among vehicles—clusters of minibuses and station wagons—holding prayer beads and a sheaf of papers in both hands. He was selling Koranic psalms, two hundred francs a sheet, Arabic lettering in black ink on newsprint. For protection on the road, he explained. Behind him waited a minibus with goods stacked high on top and bound with rope like a big, lumpy hay bale. Suitcases and bags, grain sacks, wooden boxes, and inside the van, a goat, its legs tied, shoved under a seat. I bought a psalm and folded the paper into my pocket while Issoufou settled things— bought gasoline, handled baggage, and dealt with the *komasho*, Hassan. We were going to Niamey, the capital, 540 miles west along Route 1.

Wound tight around my head and loose about neck and face, the thin cotton of my turban screened my lips. The dust, a spongy white vapor, lingered. On the roof of my mouth, a dry sediment. The capricious wind gusts seemed unable to move the vapor. No swirls, no clouds. The dust slept in even density, resilient, while the wind slapped at my hands and forehead and the earth bled into the sky. Dust masked my nose and cheeks in chalky white. Dust collected in the folds of my windbreaker; tiny, narrow drifts that startled me when I found them, as if discovering I could pinch off bits of fog.

About fifty licensed bush taxis worked Zinder's two main motor parks at that time, their union numbers painted in black over the green stripes. Station wagons, sedans, minibuses, mostly Peugeots and Toyotas. Dozens more drivers—virtually anyone else who had a car: teachers, policemen, soldiers, merchants—worked underground as unlicensed bush taxi drivers, *les chauffeurs clandestin,* either ignoring or paying off the drivers' union (Issoufou is a member) and police for the right to transport people and goods.

Issoufou worked both ways. Union drivers must wait their turn, loading passengers in the order in which they arrive in the motor parks. Issoufou did this, but he tweaked the system by working through his own discrete *komasho* network outside the park and in towns along the road. This meant that some days Issoufou was able to make a trip without ever putting his car in line at the motor park. Once in a while he made two trips. This is the way transport operates in Niger. "We survive with what we have," Issoufou said.

Issoufou never attended school. He worked six years as an accounting clerk on an agricultural research project; learned French; became bored as a government extension agent; failed as a street vendor; risked his life smuggling gasoline into Niger from oil-rich Nigeria; made a fortune; was arrested, jailed, fined; lost everything. Now he owned three bush taxis. He drove one himself and hired drivers for the other two. He gave up drinking, became a devout Muslim, joined the drivers' union and a political party, and had just taken on a second wife who was pregnant with his tenth child when we met. At last things were stable enough that he could think of going to Mecca like his father, who died there. A round-trip ticket cost about $2,500—Issoufou's take in a year—a great profit in Niger, where the per capita income is about $550.

"Transport is the only part of the economy that works now," Issoufou liked to say. "Everybody needs to travel sometime."

The Sahelien landscape of Route 1, Issoufou's physical world, lends itself to a definition of "difficult journey." Several hundred miles wide, the Sahel is wedged between tropical green to the south and the Sahara Desert to the north, stretching like a dirty bandage across Africa west to east from Senegal to Ethiopia. Every season brings its own horrors to tired land colored in shades of yellow, brown, maroon: scattered remnants of grasslands and forest, lakes of drifting sands among open laterite scabs, pockmarked volcanic rock scoured bare by wind. Rain is absent from November to March, when heat arrives like an occupying army following four months of rampage by now-cool, now-hot Harmattan winds that lunge south-west from the Sahara across the plains, carrying fine dust that strafes the skin and settles in the lungs. Harmattan is the season of meningitis, when breathing means risking death, especially for the very young. And if rain arrives in May or June, nurturing soil and crops, so will more disease. Malaria, yellow fever, cholera.

In Issoufou's car I usually took the middle-row right window seat, but that day I sat in front waiting for the motor park policeman in the black beret to complete his work. Travelers drifted in and out of the park carrying belongings on their heads. Gangs of bony little boys in dirty shorts and ragged T-shirts patrolled with begging bowls on lengths of cord tied to their necks. On the park's edges and just outside it, shopkeepers in pastel robes minded cement stalls in low buildings. A few sold cotton cloth, perfumes and music cassettes from Nigeria, used books and magazines—English and French—*Time*, *Paris-match*, cheap detective novels, romance magazines. Many merchants traded auto parts—new fan belts, rubber tubing, fuel filters, spark plugs, repair manuals. Nearby, used parts dealers sat in the dirt with goods spread on cloth or wooden tables before them. Carburetors, alternators, speedometer gauges.

I watched an old beggar man, blind and legless, clinging to the back of a boy maybe ten years old. They moved toward a long table where a man displayed auto wares—salvaged, probably, from wrecks near his village. The beggar, in a white robe folded up over his stumps, gripped the shoulders of the boy, who held his arms back to cradle the old man's torso. As the child walked, the man thrust out a tin cup and whispered in Hausa, "*Sadaka, sadaka*," a faint and squeaky plea for charity. Beggar and boy blended oddly well with the decaying cars in the streets—strips of rubber peeling off tires, bodies without doors, windows, engine hoods, or brakes. Almost all cars in Africa look this way.

It's hard not to describe scenes like these without sounding cold, exploitative, like a self-righteous neocolonial freak-show spectator. Yet the road in Niger cultivates callousness—requires it, in fact. The road is a place of casual violence and disturbing contrasts. Everyone is watching, surviving; and ironies don't go unnoticed. It was Issoufou who told me that the crippled beggars reminded him of the cars one sees everywhere, either barely functioning or abandoned. A metaphor he couldn't pass up, and neither can I. He had seen me staring at the beggars as we waited for the police official to finish with the papers.

"Their existence speaks of how we live," Issoufou said. "We always manage here. The man uses the boy's eyes and the boy uses the man's blindness. So they both eat."

The pair stopped at the table and the boy fiddled absently with a brake spring. The old man, speaking words I didn't understand, appeared to bargain for something among the carburetors and fuel filters. I saw what Issoufou was trying to tell me. The man scanned the table over the boy's shoulder, as if he hoped to find something useful: a set of eyes, a nose, a pair of used legs. The vendor handed the boy a coin; the two drifted away.

I stared after them, embarrassed at myself but still watching from my seat in the car, a source of the vendor's business. Our bad fortune helped keep him alive, but we did not need his spare parts today.

Issoufou's Peugeot 504 station wagon, or *voiture familial* (family car), as the French call a station wagon, is the bush taxi driver's car of choice. A three-ton four-cylinder moneymaker, maneuverable and fast, a good smuggling car. The 504 is to the African road what the old Soviet AK-47 automatic rifle is to rebel fighters worldwide: quick, easy, durable. It is the vehicle of the bush taxi driver and, along with the Toyota Land Cruiser, the preferred car in war. Tuareg rebels in Niger and Mali and guerrillas in Chad use Toyotas and Peugeots to attack towns, bush taxis, and military columns.

The first Peugeots, built by the French in the 1890s, were racing cars, an image that fits the 504's African legacy. In Niger and Nigeria, the Hausa call the 504 *korea mutuwa*—calabash of death. There is an even more gruesome proverb for the car: *Dufa dukka kashe bakwe kibar biyu sheda*—Cook them all, kill seven, and leave two to testify—or, in truncated form, *Dufa dukka*—Cook them all. The cabin seats seven passengers in three rows, but drivers add an eighth by packing four people across the middle seat. The car body sits low and leans forward earnestly, like a hearse, crowding the front wheels as if possessed of a mischievous need to go places. Drivers stuff baggage in a rear compartment and pile it high on the roof. Some drivers weld spare gas tanks beneath the chassis—these make a Peugeot crash brighter, more visceral. Drivers smuggle gas from Nigeria in them, and in plastic gas jugs buried beneath luggage. Roadworthy Molotov cocktails.

France's auto market has an extended second life in Africa, where many secondhand French cars, mostly Peugeots, end up. The company has a factory in Kaduna, northern Nigeria, one of a handful of automobile plants operated in sub-Saharan Africa by different companies, including Volkswagen. The Kaduna plant produces six hundred cars a month—sedans, station wagons, pickups.[1]

Regardless of the auto plants, West Africa remains a secondhand market. Today, as Tuaregs wage on-again-off-again warfare across the southern Sahara (the northern regions of Mali and Niger), a few cars still trickle across the desert carrying American and European travelers, and sometimes gun and drug traffickers. The drivers sell the vehicles for two or three times their worth in Mali, Burkina Faso, and Niger, but still cheaper than new Peugeots made in Nigeria. In the 1980s, before the Tuareg rebellion, many people made small fortunes off such cross-Sahara trips, making four or more trips a year in small fleets that sometimes included new Mercedes sedans. By the end of 1990, nearly sixty cars a week were entering Niger from Algeria, bringing in more than twelve million dollars revenue a year, according to Niger's customs service—a great deal of money in one of the world's poorest countries.

Then the Tuaregs, angered by atrocities and general mistreatment by the Mali and Niger governments, started fighting for their own piece of the Sahara. They began attacking road traffic. Rebels preyed on truck convoys and cars, infiltrating and attacking the convoys just as they had attacked Arab camel caravans for centuries. In 1992, two carloads of Tuaregs dressed as government soldiers mixed with a large group of heavy trucks on Niger's Route 2, about forty miles southwest of the ancient Saharan market city of Agadez in the north. The rebels cut off the convoy's tail, a half dozen trucks in all, including a petrol tanker and grain transports headed for Agadez, and robbed the drivers of money and as much grain as they could carry. They burned the tanker and left the drivers by their vehicles, alive.

After that, the cross-desert car market suffocated. As a result, in the early 1990s the market advantage shifted to African and European automobile dealers, who buy used cars wholesale in Europe. The cars are driven to Brussels and put aboard ships bound for the West African seaports of Dakar, Abidjan, Lome, and Cotonou. Hired drivers take the cars to countries across the West African Sahel. Used car dealers now set the prices and decide what the market will supply.

Before the rebellion, the Nigerien car market was simple. The buyer hunted for his own car, often buying directly (and more cheaply) from the owner. He sought prime spots where a decent machine might turn up. He staked out bars in tourist hotels in places like Agadez, for example, one of the first stops for trans-Saharan travelers.

Consider Issoufou Garba's experience. He bought his first car from a French tourist who began his journey in Marseilles. The Frenchman, with his wife, drove southwest through Spain, crossed the Strait of Gibraltar to Morocco by ferry, and continued southeast to Algeria. The couple headed due south over the Sahara to Agadez, where, in January 1989, they met Issoufou, who was drinking tea on a bench in the city's central market.

Issoufou bought the Frenchman's car, a 1980 Peugeot 504 station wagon in shaky condition, for four thousand dollars (around 1.2 million CFA francs at the time), more than twice the car's real value. He used money earned from smuggling Nigerian gasoline plus funds from family and friends to pay for it. (Issoufou's three Peugeots involved many investors, but he would never identify them.) The Frenchman and his wife flew back to France.

The vehicle had 130,000 miles on the speedometer, poor tires, a bad carburetor, and no working gauges. Those were the obvious problems. Issoufou installed a used carburetor but drove for six months, through a dozen flats, before he had enough money for a set of respectable used tires. Meanwhile, the car developed radiator problems. Almost all cars in Africa have this sort of convoluted history.

Driver and travelers in a Peugeot 504 pay more and take a chance on speed, on the desire to make more money and get there sooner. As I prepared to take to the road with Issoufou, I prepared mentally for a struggle of violence and wit against climate, technology, humanity, my own fears. I am drawn to the image of the early pilots, and to something the French writer and aviator Antoine de Saint Exupéry wrote in his novel *Night Flight:* "The pilot in full flight experienced neither giddiness, nor any thrill, only the mystery of metal turned to living flesh . . . he has crossed a dozen storms like lands at war."[2]

The policeman finished with Issoufou and lowered the rope across the motor park exit. As the car moved forward I smelled bitter smoke, though the dust obscured its visual presence. In Zinder, smoke rises in scattered plumes, sometimes suggesting a city under siege—buildings aflame, fighting, despair, though war and its sounds are absent. When I first arrived, I thought farmers were clearing fields by fire just beyond the city. It took me days to realize that people set roads ablaze when garbage swells in the streets.

The road from the rear of the motor park that runs past a former Renault dealership is lined with piles of goat bones and crumbling skins; orange rinds; cans; shit; bits of cloth, paper, plastic; shards of pottery, glass; a radiator grille; a piece of muffler. Nothing salvageable, always a bit of something but nothing whole, a jumbled symphony of exhausted waste crackling and hissing with the whisper of flames on wind while heat and odor twist the nostrils—the sound, sight, and smell of things falling apart.

Some days, the smoke seems to swirl around the city. Street gutters flowing with blue-green drainage from household latrines burn.

From a short distance the gutter flames seem to leap right from the earth.

The smoke contributes to a feeling, a sort of nerve gas. Silence. Fear. The speeds, drivers, predatory soldiers, ubiquitous spirits—good and bad. Demons. I think of Hell seeping playfully through the earth's crust.

Drivers at the motor park talk of benevolent spirits who serve humanity, and about dark demons, of which they speak more carefully. Such demons, I learned, live for the purpose of evil and thrive in the presence of blood—in the marketplace where butchers work, in hospitals, on the road. At the motor park, Muslim holy men, the marabouts, tell you to be careful of speech and thought because a decision not to believe may cause your death. And they sell their *gris-gris* to protect you on the road. Spiritual passports.

"The demons of the road must not be angered," a friend of Issoufou's told me at the motor park one day. "They drink the wind and laugh at the sun. They know you by the smell of your blood. They are to be feared."

I believed him. I still do.

Once, riding with Issoufou at night and traveling at great speed as usual, perhaps a hundred miles per hour, we swerved to barely miss a man, nude, standing in the road's center, his body smeared with a white paste. He stood with his feet apart, staring straight at us, and did not flinch or even appear to notice our passing. Not one of the eight passengers that night said a thing to acknowledge the event, nor did they turn to look back. No one dared, except for me. It was as if the man hadn't been there.

The next day, I asked Issoufou what he thought of the nude figure in the road and why no one had said anything. He dismissed it: "I don't know. He was just *un homme fou*"—a crazy man—"nothing to worry about." It relieved me that Issoufou did not ask me, "What man?"

Weeks later, on Route 1 a few miles east of Zinder, we slowed near a fresh accident. A minibus had rolled off the road. Smoke curled from inside the cab. I opened my door with the car still moving a little, intending to investigate, to offer help. Issoufou pulled me back with a sharp yank of my collar. "Don't you know?" he said. He reached across to shut my door. "We never go near those things. Never!"

The *gris-gris* became part of my kit, my point of view. Like my tape recorder, notebook, water bottle, and passport. I became concerned if, even for a moment, I couldn't find my amulets. The whole scenario—the road, the characters, the fear—seemed like the work of a psychopathic artist flinging paint every which way across the canvas in blinding multiple colors to see what turned up. A Jackson Pollock rendering of disaster.

Just free of the motor park, Issoufou wove his Peugeot among potholes and pedestrians, donkeys, a camel—not bothering to decrease his speed, but expecting the world to move aside for him—down a road where garbage fires did not burn. This was one of the main roads, two lanes divided by a wide dirt median. Coffee tables did business under millet-thatched shelters. You could sit on a wooden bench and buy strong, sweet Arab tea; hot Nescafé; French bread omelet sandwiches with sautéed tomatoes, garlic, onions. In Niger, such food luxuries sell where money flows, near motor parks.

I remembered first meeting Issoufou in the Zinder office of the drivers' union—le Syndicat National des Conducteurs du Niger—on this section of road, just before the strike. The office was crammed in between auto parts dealers in a long cement building. Below a chalkboard, a plywood table leaned against a wall. There I found Issoufou and two other drivers sitting and talking. Issoufou leaned forward with his elbows on the table, gesturing, as I walked through the door. I recalled the first thing I ever heard him say: *"Ahh, les militaires, ils sont tous voleurs."*—The military, they are all thieves.

Now, seated beside Issoufou in his Peugeot, I thought ahead to the first checkpoint. We emerged from the city on the road leading west, just beyond the last clusters of mud houses, approaching the rope across the road.

"Je suis Adamou Moustapha Abdourahamane, gendarme. Je suis homme. Je suis honnête!"

The gendarme, a checkpoint policeman about eighteen years old, tall and thin in olive drab and boots, stood in white desert haze between the car and the rope that hung low across the road just outside Zinder. He stood at attention, trying to click his heels in proper military fashion. He moved his right boot outward and slammed it against the left, trying for that crisp snap, glaring at Issoufou while repeating his announcement, "I am Adamou Moustapha. . . . I am a man." But Adamou was drunk, and his boot kept thudding against his ankle. Perhaps that was why he grew increasingly angry, until finally, Adamou Moustapha Abdourahamane—so fond of his full name—drew his gun. I don't recall what sort it was. Small and black. A pistol.

Automatic weapons and pistols are visible at government checkpoints in Niger, and most of West Africa. Yet, in four years of travel across a dozen African countries, I had not seen a gun, club, or knife raised in anger at a checkpoint. Occasional drunkenness, yes; verbal abuse, beatings with fists and boots: dangerous and destructive enough, to be sure, but never a drawn gun or other weapon capable of kicking off the shortcut to death.

We were at the west exit of Zinder on Route 1. I waited with the other passengers in front of the car, watching. The gendarme wanted to be sure Issoufou gave him the respect that was his due. That is part of being a gendarme, and part of checkpoint etiquette. A piece of African road culture.

In Niger, the checkpoint is itself an autonomous state, a mere line and yet a fortress. Sometimes soldiers use rope, or rags tied together, or old bicycle chains linked and hung between stakes. And I remember, from so many checkpoints, men in threadbare fatigues; their insults ("Donkey head, why are you traveling instead of plowing your fields?"); arrests; people yanked from cars because they had no identity cards, as if they threatened state security.

Adamou never deliberately aimed the pistol at anyone, but held it out inches from his right leg, his arm swaying a bit. A couple of times he raised his right hand, the gun hand, in a wobbly gesture as he talked, so that the barrel held us in its sights, if only for a second. Long enough for me to contemplate the sudden passage of a bullet through my chest. Adamou pointed the pistol now at the ground, now at his foot, and then he came back to attention holding it tight against his thigh. Mostly, though, he stared at Issoufou, who was leaning against the driver's door of his car, arms folded, studying his feet. Casual defiance. I moved slowly behind the car; some of the passengers rushed to get back inside it. But the gendarme, concentrating on Issoufou, didn't pay us any attention. His chest heaved. Anger absorbed him.

The gendarme swayed a little, taking small steps to keep his balance, holding his glare on Issoufou. He was shouting: "I, Adamou Moustapha Abdourahamane, gendarme, declare this man illegal." He raised his gun hand for a moment in Issoufou's direction, and then, as if catching himself, allowed the hand to fall heavily at his side. "His papers are incomplete and he has insulted me." Adamou stuffed the gun back into its holster (on the second try) with a deliberate thrust, like the slam of a gavel. Issoufou never looked up.

The gendarme's yelling lasted a couple of minutes and finally attracted three more gendarmes, including a sergeant. They had been playing cards on a straw mat under a tree behind the guard hut. Issoufou still leaned against the car, but now with his head flung back, studying the wispy clouds overhead. He might have been waiting for someone to change a tire. Issoufou's greatest asset was his mastery of a basic bush taxi driver's law: never let them—never let anyone—know you are upset. His apparent lack of concern probably angered Adamou more than anything else.

Our journey had reached a snag. After we pulled up to the checkpoint, Issoufou had gone into the guard hut to present the car's papers and log so they could be (as at all checkpoints) checked, stamped, dated, and signed, and to pay a bribe, another five-hundred-franc bill buried within the papers. We would have to do the same again thirty-four miles down the road, and many more times. Adamou—without looking at the car's papers, Issoufou later told me—had demanded a four-thousand-franc penalty.

Issoufou refused to pay. He walked out the door with Adamou weaving after him, reeking, we eventually realized, of whiskey (Issoufou had seen the bottle on the guard hut floor). As the two approached, Issoufou turned back to the gendarme and shrugged. He said: "*Fait comme tu veux, gendarme, mais je garde l'argent.*"— Do as you like, gendarme, but I'm keeping the money. Then he took up his silent post leaning against the car. That brought us to Adamou's speech, the heel clicking, the drawn pistol.

The incident ended with the arrival of the sergeant. Adamou saluted him (the palm-outward-fingertips-to-the-temple salute of the French military). "*Oui, mon sergent,*" Adamou shouted, pointing at Issoufou. "*C'est lui.*"—That's him. The sergeant, short and stocky with a camouflage-colored turban wrapped around his head, didn't bother to return the salute. He barked, "*Imbécile,* you're drunk again." He grabbed Adamou by the back of the neck, like a delinquent son, and propelled him, stumbling, toward the guard hut, shoved him through the door. I heard a body thud against cement and the crash of furniture falling over, but I didn't hear a sound from our antagonist, not even a groan. The other two gendarmes kept to themselves.

The sergeant returned, tucking Adamou's pistol under his belt as he walked. He carried Issoufou's car documents. I could hear his sandals slapping his feet at a brisk rhythm, a pace that betrayed a bad mood. His face was tight with disgust and his camouflage turban had come loose so that it was piled up around his neck. He handed Issoufou the log and waved his right arm impatiently, sweeping it back and forth, like a traffic officer. "*Allez, allez,* go on, get out of here."

We did. Issoufou shouted, "*Merci, chef.*" It was around 8:30 A.M. In Niger, road distances can be measured in checkpoints. We had twenty-nine to go.

Road Journal

DECEMBER 10, 1992. 10:00 A.M. On the road with Issoufou. Just Maradi and back. He wears drab, dark civil service tunic and trousers. Cotton material. Likes to chew match sticks.

Arrive Maradi 4:00 P.M. after two hours driving with full load, eight passengers. Issoufou averaged 80 mph until Tessaoua, half way, then picking up speed a little. Too fast for me, but I won't say it aloud. He concentrates on the road, leaning forward, like the body of his 504, sleeves rolled up, frowning. He seems to be barely holding the steering wheel, as if controlling it with his mind. While driving, Issoufou looks like a man doing his income tax and I feel guilty for interrupting to ask questions.

6:00 P.M. Return to Zinder. Issoufou has odd impatience behind the wheel, like most bush taxi drivers. He pulled out of the Maradi motor park doing 25 mph through market crowds of men, women, children, goats, donkeys, camels, barely stopping in time to avoid hitting an old man who was clearly disoriented, probably fresh from the village. Issoufou's frowning face never changed, never showed alarm or anger.

DECEMBER 15. Issoufou says two years ago he "saw death on the road," on haunted Route 1 section between the towns of Tchadaoua and Gazaoua, at night. He saw a "genie de la route"—a road demon that nearly made him crash. Very dark skinned woman in black cloth, carrying wood on her head, started across road in front of the car.

Issoufou: "I didn't steer around her because I would have crashed, but she just disappeared. I thought it was the devil."

DECEMBER 21. Woke up this morning after bad sleep, thinking this for some reason: Flies collect on children's faces, going to the most moist and infected spots—eyes, nose, mouth, ears—causing them to ooze yellow, exposing infection like the red dye a dentist uses to expose plaque. Vivid dream. Must be malaria pills or bad nerves. Couldn't get it out of mind, so wrote it down today at breakfast.

DECEMBER 28. Arrive Maradi 2:00 P.M. with Issoufou. Violence begins as soon as we and other bush taxis come in sight of motor park. Would-be baggage porters (street kids) and *komasho* chase us frantically, as if we are stray cattle. They open car's back hatch, pulling out baggage before Issoufou can stop. Boy swings heavy sack into another's abdomen, knocking him down, winding him. Passengers run to save belongings, unsure who is honest porter and who is a thief. Then fights start, three or four at first, then more, mostly between porters, but sometimes between porters and passengers over fees.

5:00 P.M. Want to leave, but we have only three passengers. Issoufou parks across from motor park and we wait in vehicle. Four or five illegal (clando) *komasho* force themselves on us; one gets in back seat and shouts at Issoufou. "You owe me, you owe me." Second man opens my door, muscles me over in front seat, and leans over to grab

Issoufou's wrist. He shouts: "They lie, they lie. I am the one who found the passengers." A third *komasho* leans in at Issoufou through the driver's window, his left hand gripping the wheel. "Please Issoufou, please," he says.

All of them take credit for providing three of our passengers and demand payment—1,500 francs. Issoufou calm whole time. Very impressive. Negotiates only with *komasho* named Abdou, who, from the back seat, rabbit punches face of man sitting in the front seat with me and lunges at man leaning through the window. Both men leave. Abdou is satisfied. I have met Abdou twice now and am used to his methods. He grins, says to me: "These people, they are all crazy. Never trust anyone." Issoufou pays Abdou 700 francs. We go, hoping to find more passengers in road villages.

They seemed a confused assortment of different
human parts. It occurred to me that they were spirits
who had borrowed bits of human beings to partake of
human reality. They say spirits do this sometimes.
— Ben Okri, *The Famished Road*

Waiting for the Marabout

Issoufou Garba and I talked in his home while the wind blew hard, cooling the air and blurring it with dust that hung gently in the room. The temperature was around sixty degrees, normal for December in Niger. Issoufou wore a turtleneck shirt beneath his regular dark blue tunic and a long-sleeved T-shirt. After I arrived he added a frayed brown woolen sweater. He wore his trousers under old blue nylon sweatpants, white socks with his sandals, and a gray turban wrapped tightly around his head. Not Issoufou's normal garb, but this was winter. Midseason for the Harmattan winds.

Issoufou had arranged this evening in seriousness, though he joked about it. "Tonight we continue your education."

We were waiting for Malam Shafi, a teacher and holy man of some renown. A marabout. Part Muslim priest and part magician. The Hausa also use the word *malam* as a formal title for a teacher of distinction. "When do you expect him?" I asked.

Issoufou shrugged. "He said tonight, *Inch' Allah.*"—God willing. Understanding that it could be some time, I settled in to listen and learn. His eight-year-old son brought us tea. It was around 8:00 P.M.

We sat at a metal table in the main room of the house, a large square mud building with four rooms and a cement patio in a compound surrounded by six-foot mud walls to protect against thieves. A French translation of the Koran lay on the table in front of a stack of books: a French language dictionary, an old Peugeot manual, a couple of slim paperbacks, a Dick Francis mystery in French, and a prayer book called *Les noms les plus exaltés d'Allah* (The most exalted names of Allah). Issoufou did not aspire to be a marabout, but he took pride in his knowledge of spiritual matters.

He said, "On the road, it is not only people you must fear. There are many sources of evil and danger." I saw an opportunity and asked him to explain some things: the plastic disk that hung by a cord from his rear-view mirror, for one. The disk was embossed with gold Arabic lettering reading "God go with us." On the rear window were stickers bearing the same wording. In the upper right corner of the windshield was the photo of a Nigerien imam, a high priest of Islam, in flowing white robe and turban.

As a professional bush taxi driver, Issoufou belonged to a special class of road traveler in Africa. Niger's roads are its lifeline to the world. Niamey, the capital city, has an airport, but there is no national airline, no railroad. The Niger River flows along the country's western edge, useless to most of Niger's nine million people. Foreign relief workers, diplomats, and tourists depend on the benevolence of Air France and Air Afrique to keep Niamey as a stopover on flights to Paris from regional capitals. Everyone else looks to the bush taxi driver, whose relationship to the road is intensely spiritual.

"They are *gris-gris,* aren't they," I said to Issoufou.

Issoufou smiled. "You are beginning to understand."

Gris-gris are hard to miss on Niger's roads. You see them painted on trucks and cars, on stickers plastered on almost every vehicle, a salad of proverbs and slogans in English, French, Arabic, and Hausa. I kept a running list of them—translated to English—in a separate notebook: "Allah Is My Co-Pilot"; "No Fear of Death"; "That which is done well is never lost"; "No King is God"; "Don't crowd me, I drive with Jesus"; and my favorite: "This is God's bush taxi."

In most societies, people cling to a hope that fate can be managed, even cheated. In Niger, a tailor hangs *gris-gris* on his sewing machine for business success; a prostitute wears a *gris-gris* belt for protection against disease. In Mexico, bus drivers cover their vehicles—windows, dashboard, bumpers, and hood—with pictures and statues of the Virgin Mary. In India, motorists adorn cars with ornate images of Hindu deities. American motorists use similar icons, if less frequently and with less passion. A few of us fix plastic statues of a patron saint to the dashboard.

But a deeper awareness of fate and vulnerability to a powerful spiritual world permeates daily life in West Africa. This is certainly true in Niger, where the population is more than 90 percent Muslim and an automobile is a once-in-a-lifetime possession, hard-won and easily lost to breakdown or accident. Nigeriens tend to blame misfortune on God's will or the work of demons. Control, for many people, is not a spoken part of life's equation. To overtly desire control is to challenge God's will. In a place such as this where money, materials, and basic necessities are lacking, *gris-gris* are tools of control, though they are not thought of that way. *Gris-gris* are a kind of spiritual insurance policy.

At home, I identify an American friend's car by its make and color, a telltale dent or rust mark, maybe a bumper sticker. I recognized Issoufou's car by its many *gris-gris*, and because he was the only driver who kept a milkweed branch tied to his side-view mirror ("Demons find its odor unpleasant").

When I bought two *gris-gris* from a marabout in a local market, Issoufou did not approve. "The marabouts of the marketplace are charlatans," he told me. "That man stole your money. You must let me introduce you to a proper marabout." Malam Shafi, he said, was a great marabout who came from a family of marabouts in a village near Zinder. Issoufou promised a meeting. So that windy evening at his home we waited and talked.

I am wary of religion. My boyhood in a Catholic family was marked by my resentment of church authority and a skepticism fed by unanswered questions. When I was twelve, my catechism instructor declared my brother's marriage to a Protestant woman invalid "in the eyes of God." Pressed by confusion into insubordination, I asked her why God would object. "You should already understand," she said. I wanted reasons and asked for a biblical reference to justify her claim. "I shouldn't have to offer you evidence," she added, as if the logic were obvious. The remark humbled me to silence. I was to understand what? From my lessons I understood that I was under surveillance by "the Holy Spirit," who knew my hatreds, my jealousies, and every time I swore or masturbated. I lived in confusion and guilt.

In second grade, during my brief attendance in a Catholic school, I saw a nun slap a classmate for a dress code violation, a stray shirttail. What justified the violence? Where was God's "all-encompassing love"? In college I roomed with a student so scarred from years in a Catholic academy that he could not function socially. And later, while visiting Dachau, the former Nazi death camp, I could not comprehend how any faith could insist, in the face of such evil, on belief in God's omniscient power and compassion. If he exists, I thought, certainly he is cynical.

In my own culture, I feel comfortable enough to openly challenge my religious faith. In Africa, however, I sensed a fear so deep that people dare not raise questions. Nonbelief is too great a risk. Even Islam and Christianity—comparative latecomers in Africa's religious history—cannot overcome the continent's complex web of spiritual values dating back tens of thousands of years. Many Nigerien marabouts profess Islamic teachings while accommodating traditional beliefs that attribute powers to animals, plants, and forces of nature in defiance of Islam's insistence that God alone controls all elements, all spiritual forces.

In his book *Niger: Personal Rule and Survival in the Sahel,* Robert Charlick, a Cleveland State University political scientist who has studied Niger since the 1960s, notes that "Nigeriens have been Islamized for only a very short time." He adds, "Not only have they retained many pre-Islamic practices (particularly cults of spirit possession or 'bori'), but they have yet to fully accept the radically different understanding of the world that Islam brings.... Old values and social structures . . . die hard."[1]

Once, on a newspaper assignment in Ivory Coast, where Islam and Christianity mix freely with traditional beliefs, I talked with Professor Georges Niangoran-Bouah, an anthropologist from the University of Abidjan. The writer V. S. Naipaul had sought Professor Niangoran-Bouah out during a 1982 journey to Ivory Coast, chronicled in the essay "The Crocodiles of Yamoussoukro." The professor told Naipaul that "there are people in the villages today who can give you news every night of Paris and Russia. And they are certainly not getting it on the radio."[2] When I spoke to Professor Niangoran-Bouah, he stressed his view that Africans and Europeans view spiritual issues very differently. "White people talk about going to the moon," he told me. "That is nothing. Here people speak of journeys of a few minutes between continents; they speak of powers that transcend the machines you've developed. I, too, am skeptical, but listen to this. I once met a man in his village who told me he'd gone the night before to visit his son who was studying in Canada. He talked in great detail about the place where his son lived, what his son had done that evening, what he wore and had for dinner, all details the son verified later. He told me he had never discussed those things with his father. How does one explain this?" The professor shrugged at his own question. Telephones, he assured me, were not involved.

By the time I met Professor Niangoran-Bouah, I'd seen enough in Africa to respect what I could not explain. Once, while walking through a village in Niger, I encountered a young woman lying unconscious on her back. She wore a soiled wraparound cloth, and her face and limbs were caked in white paste. She appeared to be asleep, but when I knelt to investigate, villagers rushed from their homes and pulled me away. "Don't touch her," they told me. They said she had wandered in from another village during the night, screaming and yelling like someone out of her mind. Then she collapsed. The woman, the people insisted, was possessed and must not be handled lest the demons inside her be angered. "*Monsieur, faites attention. C'est le diable!*"—which literally means, "Be careful, it's the devil," but which I interpreted as, "Be careful, the devil is in her." She was, to them, spiritually contagious. Wherever I went I was impressed and disturbed by the intensity of belief I saw. I had never been exposed to spiritual faith so profound that it ruled how people did business, ate, slept, made love, and traveled.

In Africa, you learn to live with the demon world. Demons keep reality in check. You learn never to ask after the purpose of *gris-gris* (to hide their secret from demons) or a child's well-being (jealous spirits might rob it of its health). A mother does not wipe flies away from a child's eyes because the action might attract a demon's attention. You grow used to paranoia and stories about black spirits that kill with a glance. On the road, demons explain why certain parts of the highway—a sharp curve, a steep hill—are more dangerous, or why more accidents happen at night. Life is spooky. To preserve my peace of mind, I respected these things even if I couldn't openly profess a belief in them. Neither can I tell anyone even now that I disbelieve the power of marabouts and demons.

I recognized, as well, a spiritual connection in the way the odd and insane live openly in Africa, ignored but uneasily respected. The underlying fear is that they understand a world the rest of us don't see. To me, they were harmless crazies on a continent whose impoverished medical services offer little psychiatric care. When I voiced that idea, Nigeriens advised me to speak more carefully because "the crazies" might be people of great understanding—able to converse with the wind, to zip off to distant continents inside a peanut shell—and they might be listening. In Niamey, a young man wanders the streets solving complex multiplication, calculus, and algebra problems on demand, for a few coins. He is not crazy, but odd, a savant who calls himself "The Calculator." He does each problem in seconds, accurately. And he is starving.

On another level of the bizarre, in the open markets marabouts spread out their wares on burlap: curses, spells, *gris-gris*. They sit beside women who sell vegetables and grains, and other women who sell pills, some fake and some real, on the medical black market. The women arrange the pills in piles: aspirin, cough lozenges, orange pills for sexual longevity, red pills for poor eyesight, white ones for colds. The marabouts, too, arrange their wares in little piles. They display stacks of Korans in French, Arabic, and English; and tiny prayer books or collections of Muslim proverbs. Beside the literature there are powders pounded from bits of wood and bone—the bark of a gao, the tusk of an elephant, the teeth of a lion. The powders cure disease and impotence, protect you from enemies. The skull of a vulture, the dried corpse of a chameleon, the skins of vipers and cobras, various herbs. A psychosomatic public pharmacy.

As we waited for the marabout, I pressed Issoufou to talk about Islam's connection to roads and demons. He reminded me of one of the basic powers attributed to Satan by Muslims and Christians alike—the belief that Satan can assume any form. The marabouts, Issoufou explained, warn that Satan can take as many forms as he likes—any time, any place. I had found the Koran to be vague about Satan's power, neither acknowledging nor denying the existence of demon forms of Satan, though his deceptive powers are well emphasized. Both Islam and Christianity accept the story of the .emptation in the Garden of Eden and see Satan in the image of the serpent. I told Issoufou of my doubts. He picked up his Koran and showed me the sixty-ninth sura, or chapter, which contains a warning to the faithful to recognize "the Sure Reality" and not false appearances. This means, Issoufou explained, that one must be wary of evil, of Satan himself, lurking in an apparently normal idea, action, or image. Then Issoufou pointed to various references to the "jinn," invisible forces or spirits of good and evil. We read sura 15: "And the jinn race, We had Created before, from the fire of a scorching wind." At night in the bush, Issoufou said, you can see the demons as tongues of fire darting about on missions known only to them. Then he turned to sura 72, which reveals that jinn work in God's favor, and also against him. "There are among us some that are righteous and some the contrary." The conversation and interpretations went on until the Koran itself seemed irrelevant. You run with your own interpretations.

The winter wind rattled the iron roof above us. Issoufou continued in his own words. "Along the roads the demons have their villages from which they prey on travelers. They have villages here in the city and in the fields." Listening to this, I found it useful not to worry whether a belief or legend had a corresponding reference in the Koran. Issoufou added, "In the bush, farmers must consult the marabouts about where they plant their seeds. Crops planted on demon territory are poisonous. They will wilt. If you eat from the fields you will die."

"Demon villages?"

"Oh, yes," he said. "You can't see them, but you can find evidence of their work on the sections of the road where there are more wrecks than usual, between Zinder and Takiéta, for instance. You and I have traveled that road several times."

I had counted seventeen wrecks on that thirty-three-mile section of Route 1, most of them completely burned out and scattered about the roadside like huge chunks of charcoal. Issoufou called such sections of road by a Hausa term: *Hanya mai iska*, which means "road of the wind," or, more plainly, "haunted road." Four such sections exist between Zinder and Maradi; there are dozens along the entire length of Route 1.

"*C'est comme la chasse*," Issoufou told me—It's like hunting. "The demons always search for the driver who is unsure of himself. They find the ones who are scared. Somehow they just know them. It's easiest for the demons at night when there is so much fear on the road. The demons are more powerful at night." I thought of the gendarme commander in Niamey who told me that more than three quarters of the accidents on Route 1 happen at night. Once I heard an American relief worker in Niamey say: "*Driving in Africa at night can make you crazy. People don't replace burned out headlights, and you see people along the road in the darkness, wandering crazies, like zombies, it's nuts!*"

Issoufou continued. "The marabouts teach us that demons are attracted to places of blood, like where animals are slaughtered in the markets and on the roads, where blood is often spilled; and they are known to follow herds of animals, like cows, goats, camels, and donkeys, which alone can see them and hear what demons say. Demons inhabit their minds. You see, that's why animals are always wandering onto the road, just in front of a car."

The reasoning gave me an idea. Wandering livestock pose a great hazard on the road, night or day. I said, "It's as if someone were whispering in the animal's ear, 'Go on, go ahead, nothing will hurt you.' Like temptation from the devil."

Issoufou smiled. "If you like. The marabout can tell you more."

There is more to the power of marabouts.

In 1987, Niger's late ruler, General Seyni Kountché, died of a brain tumor, leaving his cousin, a lieutenant colonel, to rule. Students protested the corruption and human rights violations. Some were shot; some died. The army lost popular respect, and the lieutenant colonel announced a program of transition to civilian government. Civilian leaders held a national convention in the summer of 1991 to write a new constitution, set elections, and investigate the past sixteen years of military rule. They appointed a group of bureaucrats, educators, and village chiefs to a Commission of Crimes and Abuses.

Common people, officers, and former ministers testified at long tables on the basketball court of the Seyni Kountché National Stadium. Farmers insulted generals and colonels; colonels, majors, and captains accused each other of conspiracy and murder. Officials testified about the Bureau de la Liaison et de la Coordination, Kountché's secret police, whose informers reported anyone who showed the regime the slightest disrespect. People had gone to prison for frowning at Kountché's photograph in public places. The general was disgraced, his image of austere integrity ruined. And Kountché's successor, the lieutenant colonel, allowed himself to fade into the background.

Then things got weird.

Amadou "Bonkano" Oumarou, former chief of the secret police and leader of a failed coup against Kountché, returned from exile in Europe to testify—in exchange for immunity—before the commission. He announced that he held all of Kountché's secrets, that Kountché, his mental control slipping in the early 1980s, had been obsessed with the occult. Bonkano, son of a family of clairvoyants, referred to himself as Kountché's former spiritual adviser, as a marabout. Policy was formed and heads of state received, Bonkano claimed, on a foundation of paranoia, depending on the advice of marabouts. And he, Bonkano, who had mastered the Koran at thirteen, who had traveled the world to study the occult, was the link between General Kountché and the marketplace of superstition.

Bonkano played the eager witness impatient to please his civilian inquisitors (by denouncing Kountché) and build up his own image. "I know many types of marabouts," Bonkano told Niger's independent newspaper *Haské*: "There are those who help women give birth and predict the child's destiny; there are those who help women find husbands; and there are the great marabouts who can make you 'someone great.' There are all kinds."[3]

Bonkano's coup collapsed when some officers decided to remain loyal to Kountché, and Bonkano—a man with no formal education, illiterate in French while in Kountché's service—escaped to a comfortable exile in Belgium. On his return to Niger, Bonkano the commission witness became a folk hero, the gods' link to the dictator, a gadfly who said he once controlled thousands of Soviet and American secret agents around the world—*the world*—in Kountché's name. Bonkano paid them and himself, he said, with money from the national treasury, money that came from the uranium mines in the northeast and stolen foreign aid funds.

In city and village markets all along the length of Route 1, Bonkano's deep, steady nasal voice floated at high volume from bootleg tapes of his appearance before the commission. "Listen well, for what I have to tell you is very important, *aahhh oui, très important*." Bonkano's recorded voice looped, twisted, and stuttered with every claim. "In the name of God and the Republic I'm going to explain to you everything. . . . I had millions." The voice stabbed through car windows, stopping passersby in the street, boasting of power and riches. "I built villas. . . . I had under me six thousand Soviet secret agents and seven thousand Americans, *aahh ouii, aahh ouii, c'est vrai, je dis.*" Bonkano continued talking until all the testimony, its weave of truths and lies, blended into a kind of infectious nerve gas. "We spent enormously. We dealt with all the great marabouts. . . . Kountché needed them to be the supreme leader. If you didn't believe in them, you couldn't stay with Kountché."[4] You could hear in his voice the greed that motivated him to seek power for himself.

In different circumstances, the story might be just a little amusing, somewhat embarrassing, like Nancy Reagan's astrologer or Richard Nixon's plea to Henry Kissinger to kneel with him and pray as his presidency collapsed. Bonkano's tale would be forgettable, even strangely quaint, were not the whole scene so pathetic and tragic. But in Niger, where 60 percent of the population is under the age of sixteen, starvation is a rite of passage through childhood; civil servants go unpaid for months; the cost of road accidents rivals the national budget.

"Bonkano is our little clown," Issoufou said one day as we stood in the Maradi motor park listening to Bonkano's voice on a tape vendor's cassette player. "He makes great theater, but he wasted so much." Issoufou told me he'd heard a rumor that marabouts in Niamey were making huge sums off politicians seeking extra help in the upcoming elections. He laughed. "I'm sure Bonkano the great marabout is getting rich."

Indeed, Bonkano's testimony helped to destroy Kountché's reputation, but Bonkano walked away a free man, a joke to some and a spiritual hero to others. The commission could charge him with nothing, nor did its members declare whether or not they took Bonkano's testimony seriously. He lives in Niamey today, leading the life of a spiritual consultant, Niger's most expensive marabout.

The National Archives in Niamey contain much more information about marabouts. I sifted through thousands of pages of fraying colonial documents in cardboard cartons stacked on rows of metal shelves. The papers reveal that the French saw a subversive threat in the power of the marabouts. They grudgingly acknowledged the marabouts' importance and tried to control them, to keep tabs on them. They studied the marabouts, recording their findings in neat typescripts, in triplicate carbon copies on onionskin. There are long reports and numbered lists of marabouts by name, village, and region printed in straight, narrow columns. The French interviewed marabouts, spied on them, and ranked them by the number of devotees they claimed. Then they filed all the information away, with copies sent to the territorial governor in Niamey, the colonial governor-general in Dakar, and the Maritime Ministry in Paris. Few French officials learned the languages the marabouts spoke—Hausa, Zarma, Arabic, or any other indigenous language. Occasionally they threw marabouts in jail for sedition or "*maraboutage*," holding them responsible for localized problems or rebellions: a village that fell behind in grain taxes, a chief who refused to surrender village men for forced labor on the roads.

The French harbored a permanent contempt for Islam, viewing it as a religion poisoned by superstition and represented by the "empty" and "corrupt" power of the marabouts, who would guarantee fulfillment of any wish for a price. Lieutenant Mathey, Zinder's district commandant in 1944, wrote his superiors: "Practiced Islam is burdened by charlatanism, which carefully supports some marabouts through the sale of amulets."[5]

The evening approached 9:00 P.M. Issoufou asked me what I understood of demons. I'd done some reading, I said. I'd read the Koran, some anthropology, had talked to drivers and a couple of anthropologists who had studied demons. Among the things I'd read was a book, written in French, called *Le monde mystérieux des chasseurs traditionnels* (The mysterious world of traditional hunters), by the Nigerien anthropologist Keletigui Abdourahamane Mariko, one of West Africa's most prominent historians and cultural observers. By "traditional hunter" Mariko means not a hunter of animals, but a hunter of the spirit who survives through a special awareness of people and animals and of the spiritual nature of his natural environment. "He is in permanent communion with invisible forces, the masters of nature," Mariko writes, adding: "For him there are two forces always present: the spirits who will work with him for a few sacrifices, and the bad spirits who do only evil to those who violate their domains."[6]

Issoufou pulled a thin paperback from the stack of books on his desk. "Have you seen this?" he asked. The book was a collection of Mariko's poems, published in France and entitled *Poèmes sahéliens en liberté*. He read part of a poem called "Mystérieuse Afrique":

Mysteries and superstitions everywhere
Even during the night, the shepherds' dogs
Bark against the hyenas of the dead
Howling at death . . .
Africa, the African spirit, birthplace of nocturnal mysteries
Of the fear of sorcerers, eaters of the spirit
Remaining for us something unknown.[7]

Issoufou put down the book. "These 'eaters of the spirit' are the black spirits," he said. "I think that's what Mariko is talking about. They are different forms of the devil and they exist to do evil." He paused and added, "You must remember this—the devil can take any form but that of the Prophet himself."

I had to ask Issoufou something more. "What do these demons look like when they are in their own form? Or do they even have their own form?"

Issoufou frowned at the question. "Wait for the marabout," he said. "He is the kind of hunter Mariko speaks of."

Malam Shafi arrived at ten. Issoufou gave him the best seat, a dirty sofa whose fabric had ripped away from the foam rubber. The marabout's long, dust-stained robe fell to his feet. The white cotton had blurred to brown, with dark spots where dust had stuck to moisture from food or water fallen from his lips. Around his shoulders he wore a dirty tan burlap shawl, badly frayed. He had buttoned his robe tightly around his neck. The old man didn't seem bothered by the cold. Even I had on two shirts, a sweater, and a turban, which was hanging loose around my neck. Malam Shafi's feet, sheathed in peeling and cracked leather sandals, were aged and weathered more than the smooth skin of his face. He was very thin and walked slowly.

The marabout said he had walked to Zinder the day before from his house in the bush, twenty-one miles to the south. He was accustomed to foot travel, moving from village to hamlet to village to city answering calls for his services. The skin around the soles of his feet was chalky brown, deeply ridged with vertical cracks, and dry, as if petrified. His yellowed toenails were scrunched and twisted. He sat still, a wooden cane leaning between his knees. I guessed he was in his seventies, though Issoufou did not know his age. Somehow Malam Shafi did not seem like a poor man, but rather a man unconcerned with appearances, a man who did not need money.

He smiled a lot but didn't speak French. Issoufou acted as interpreter, introducing me and explaining, in Hausa, why I wanted to see him. Issoufou talked for several minutes. Then Malam Shafi abruptly became serious. He started talking as if scolding me, looking now at Issoufou and now at me to see if I understood him.

"Only a few marabouts have seen demons," he said, through Issoufou. "They take moisture from the eyes of a dog and anoint their own eyes with it in order to gain the temporary power, but it's very dangerous, and they don't talk about it. I have never seen demons in their true form and never want to. I don't know anyone who has seen what they look like. I do know a marabout who went crazy when he tried." The concept stunned me—the notion that moisture from a dog's eyes can provide a temporary lens to view another world.

"Don't worry," I tried to say in Hausa. "I really don't want to see one of these things." The idea, like so much of the demon lore I was hearing, both disturbed and attracted me. It fueled a voyeuristic thrill, but not so much that I wanted to try it. The marabout smiled a little. I didn't ask for a demonstration of his powers, for proof that they were real, although perhaps I should have. That would have seemed cheap.

I asked Malam Shafi if road travel scared him. He smiled. "Not at all," he said. "The demons do not bother me."

"What about the gendarmes?"

Issoufou looked at me. "He doesn't need identity papers." I pressed the question. "Ask him why."

"The gendarmes never notice me," the marabout said. "They never ask for my papers or even talk to me. I travel freely."

"How is that possible?"

Issoufou, annoyed that I seemed to be challenging the marabout, continued to translate anyway. Malam Shafi smiled at me and shrugged. There was a pause. "He protects himself," Issoufou said. Then the marabout, serious again, began a brief monologue that I did not understand.

Issoufou turned to me. "He thinks that what you're doing is dangerous. He says the road shouldn't be studied." The comment made me sit back. I didn't know what to say, but the old man filled the silence. He interrupted in Hausa:

"One who is on the road is always at risk," he said. "You must take care to be safe."

"Safe from the road?"

"No," he said. "From the demons who inhabit the road. You know they are present when you see something very strange or when you experience a brief fever. The road itself is not the spirit, it is the innocent host."

Malam Shafi's warning not to study the road bothered me. The more I listened, the more worried I became. After a while he pulled a leather amulet from a pocket in his robe. He took my right hand between his hands and pressed the object into my palm. This was the first of three *gris-gris* he gave me that night. Each amulet was eyeball sized and bound in red leather with a leather cord attached so it could be worn around the neck. The first was to protect me on the road; the second was for my health; the third was for general good luck.

He said: "Wear them or keep them in pockets individually, separated from each other and everything else, especially money. With these, you will travel without problems." Issoufou's son brought a tray with three shot glasses of strong, sweet tea. I took one. The marabout continued. "You will encounter no problems where the path of a wrongdoer crosses yours. And as long as you use them, you must also remain chaste."

I paid close attention to his instructions, which, Issoufou later told me, were meant to protect the sacred power and dignity of the *gris-gris*. Contact with money, for example, would soil them, or worse. "If you don't treat the *gris-gris* with respect," Issoufou said, "they might work against you. You must understand that. And do not assume that they belong to you. They are the property of God. That's very important."

I gave Malam Shafi six thousand francs, which pleased him. He smiled broadly and shook my hand and Issoufou's. He accepted another glass of tea. We talked awhile longer about the dangers of the road, and he assured me once again that I would be safe. "I know this," he said.

Right away I put one *gri-gri* around my neck, one in an empty pocket of my shoulder bag, and another in a shirt pocket. I spread them out, in other words, to maximize their coverage. Even as I sat in Issoufou's home that night, those tiny leather spheres both comforted and unnerved me, as if I had gained a small measure of security but surrendered something of my core in exchange. They challenged my sense of fate, my assumption of ultimate responsibility for how my life unfolds. To carry the *gris-gris* was to confess belief in a parallel world. Yet in the face of the road's realities, the high-speed dangers and omnipresent visual reminders of death, I was ready to accept anything that would help me endure. In fact, I was grateful for the *gris-gris* and protected them. I didn't tell anyone about them, and I never went out without making certain they were safely on my person.

A week later, riding with Issoufou in his bush taxi, I would experience a moment of real fear when I thought the amulet I had put in my bag was lost. I searched frantically and finally found it between pages of my notes. I was breathing hard, startled by my fear at the thought of losing my protection against something I had been told not to study. From the driver's seat, Issoufou looked at me. "Forgot something?" he asked. I smiled and said it was my notebook, but I had found it. For a moment, in the middle of that lie, I felt like an addict.

At the end of the evening, Issoufou accompanied Malam Shafi to the compound door and spoke to him for a few minutes in low tones. Issoufou had asked me to stay in the house because he wanted to talk to the marabout alone. From the doorway, I saw Issoufou take something from him, and I guessed he was negotiating for his own *gris-gris*. When Issoufou returned, he said, "Malam Shafi is going to

Niamey tomorrow. He told me the colonel has called for his help."
Two former army colonels had entered the presidential race, and I
asked Issoufou which one had hired Malam Shafi. Issoufou shrugged.
"Does it matter?"

The motive of a journey deserves little attention.
It is not the fully conscious mind which chooses
West Africa in preference to Switzerland.
— Graham Greene, *Journey without Maps*

Zinder Notes

I needed, after a few weeks sharing a car with Issoufou Garba, to drink in order to sleep. Evenings, wherever we ended up, I downed three 1.5-liter bottles of Biére Niger, a product of the national brewery. I drank mostly in village bars, where they cooled the beer in a damp pit covered by wet cloth. In Zinder, I went to the Hotel Central bar, with its prostitutes from southern Nigeria and one regular customer, a despondent soldier. Every night he leaned on the bar, automatic rifle propped against the stone countertop, quietly sipping his beer and talking to no one. I drank without Issoufou, whose Muslim faith forbade him to use alcohol. I never got drunk, only tired enough to sleep. I was too wired, I suppose, to become giddy.

I had a room at a hostel, which was the large home of a Zinder family who rented space to travelers. Mornings I walked to the motor park coffee table popular with drivers, including Issoufou. We waited for passengers, drank coffee—instant Nescafé canned in Ivory Coast—told stories, exchanged news. We found out who had crashed or broken down, who had been in trouble at checkpoints and how much it had cost them, which driver had been arrested or beaten. "You heard about Moussa?" someone asked. "Salif says he hit a bull yesterday near Tessaoua. He still hasn't come back."

The coffee table scene was like a mission debriefing: checking off goals, tallying casualties. Cars, like shot-up aircraft, limped back from someplace—Agadez, Nguigmi, Diffa, Maradi, Kano, Niamey, bush villages—every hour, chewed up and spit out by the road. The image of the West African motor park and its legions of beat-up cars and drivers suggests a conflict with the unknowable. I think again of Saint Exupéry, who wrote of a pilot's struggle against the elements: "It isn't the individual that's responsible, but a sort of hidden force."[1]

Issoufou Garba wanted to see a Mad Max movie, *Beyond Thunderdome,* at the Hotel Central theater, an outdoor courtyard where a man projects movies on a whitewashed wall. He invited me to join him. The idea of seeing Tina Turner on a big screen, larger than life, pleased him. "It's Tina," Issoufou said, sitting that morning at the coffee table. "We're going to see Teeena tonight."

At 8:00 P.M. men packed the theater, which normally shows Kung Fu movies, French police dramas, Hindu love stories. I shared a long wooden bench with Issoufou and a half dozen other drivers wearing simple cotton robes or leisure-style African business suits in shades of gray, navy blue, brown. They laughed a little conspiratorially, a little nervously, looking about the place with arms folded. There was, after all, some guilt involved. These men, supporters of wives and children (at least thirty-five children between them), had paid the three-hundred-franc entry fee, money that could buy a family enough rice for a couple of days. But this was a road movie, a way for drivers to fantasize—about Tina Turner, yes, but about themselves as well. They wanted to see the last scene, the surreal, apocalyptic road battle fought in the Australian desert at high speed with homemade automobile hybrids—reinvented cars that functioned in a brutal, cynical, decayed, post–nuclear war desert world very similar to the scenario around them, subtracting nuclear war.

I watched, expecting something to happen—wild shouting, perhaps, some sort of road culture audience participation; cheers, maybe. Yet my companions sat and looked on politely, silently enthralled for an hour and a quarter, until the road chase, when Mel Gibson's character climbs from one vehicle to another. Then I heard gasps, laughs, sounds of excited approval: *"Oooh la, la, c'est pas vrai ça,"* or a slightly drawn out *"Alllahh!"* or *"Monnn Dieu!"* or the sharp Hausa exclamation, *"Kai!"*

On the way out, a driver named Mamane asked me, half joking, half seriously: "Is it that way in America?"

I liked the Hotel Central because, in an old Muslim market city and sultanate, the hotel represents vice like a quiet bordello in the Vatican. Long verandahs with low cement arches frame two sides of a gravel courtyard; behind each arch is a door to an empty room, twelve in all. At the courtyard's far end is a half-circle stone bar under a millet-thatch awning. Next door, high white cement walls enclose the outdoor theater. In Zinder—where I saw men publicly beat and stone women who did not cover their heads with cloth as the imams required, where in the summer of 1992 a mob of men burned the offices of a women's center—the Hotel Central offered me sanctuary from events in a city that sometimes appeared to be going mad.

The motor park is next door to the hotel, which seemed to me a natural extension of that world. Carnival manifestations of the road wash up in front of those white walls: the occasional road movie, a traveling automobile spectacle. One day, two German used car dealers arrived from Cotonou (Benin) in two eighteen-wheelers loaded with used Peugeot 504 sedans and station wagons recently offloaded from freighters that had sailed from Brussels.

"Karl" and "Walter," as the prostitutes called the Germans, wore jeans with cowboy boots and brown leather vests over T-shirts. For three weeks they hung out between the bar and their rooms, where they negotiated with buyers and spent nights with the barmaids, the only other people they seemed to know. Karl was thin, balding, with a wispy red beard, sunken cheeks and eyes, quivering hands. At the bar he held his beer with two hands. He had on a stiff, new brown fedora with a brown leather band. I tried talking to him one night.

"I'm told you're selling cars."

He looked at me, folding his arms. "Got a cigarette?" he asked.

"Sorry."

He looked at me again, up and down. I was at least as scrawny as he was, at least as hollow faced, and, apparently, unable to hide the fact I had no intention of buying a car. In crisp English, he said, "Run along little doggy." Karl sipped his beer, and I shrugged and walked away.

Souley, the old hotel barman, later told me, "They sell more than cars." He raised both fists and put them together to make the staccato sound and movement of automatic weapons: "*Ta-ta-ta-ta-ta-ta.* Guns, guns."

At the coffee table, I told Issoufou the story. It became his favorite. Two or three times a day he slowly repeated my imitation of Karl's English, "Run a-long leetle doggy," and laughed.

Some mornings Issoufou sent me on spare parts errands, normally the job of a *karamota.* The apprentice mechanic, usually a boy between ten and eighteen, races like a dog after the machine he works on (usually a minibus) has started moving, and then jumps in a side or rear door. Once inside, the *karamota*—"dog of the car"—crouches with his back against the closed door. For my errands, the drivers awarded me the honorary Hausa nickname "Anasara karamota."

Anasara, a term derived from Arabic, means something like "Christian," and the Hausa use it as a name for white people.

Often we didn't leave until evening.

Days came when I felt used to the road. On others I was sick and frightened. I never told Issoufou.

One evening, a crowd of men gathered around a brightly lit platform in a sandy lot outside the Hotel Central. Mounted on the platform was a two-door compact Renault with oversized tires like a dune buggy. The car sat inside a blue steel frame that wrapped around it like a big claw, bolted to the top and sides. An amusement park ride. On the hotel wall hung a giant blue-and-white cloth poster with "Rothman's"—a popular French cigarette brand—printed in blue across the center. The same letters stretched across both sides of the car.

A Frenchman in tight jeans and sneakers stood on the platform. He had thick brown hair and a beard, and he wore a white Rothman's T-shirt that struggled to hold in his belly. Holding a microphone, he leaned back against the driver's door, blank-faced as he read from a paper, his voice nearly lost in static. A tall, bone-thin young man in dark trousers and shirt pushed his way to the front, holding high a blue raffle ticket. He'd apparently won a drawing. The man pulled him by the hand onto the platform and pushed him to the car. The young man got behind the wheel and waited as the Frenchman, cigarette hanging from his lips, buckled and snapped straps across the winner's torso and thighs. The Frenchman shut the door and walked to the rear of the platform, to a small box bolted to the metal frame holding the car, pressed several buttons, pulled a lever, and jumped into the sand. He glanced at his watch and walked into the bar.

The frame's hydraulic arms slowly lifted the vehicle off the platform and tilted the car nose-up as the winner, his face revealed by the glow of an inside light, stared straight ahead, hands gripping the wheel. His expression was nil, like someone struggling to maintain his youthful male dignity in a moment of bewilderment.

There came a hydraulic hissing and the car suddenly began rolling up and down, quickly but not violently, as if climbing and descending a succession of small steep hills or desert dunes. All this happened within the firm grip of the hydraulic frame. No automobile engine sound, just hissing and whirring. The car, of course, never left the platform. It dipped to one side and then the other, like a vehicle rounding a hillside, before straightening into a spasm of violent shaking in sharp little jerks, mimicking movement on a bumpy road. The crowd of about two hundred men and boys watched patiently, coldly, for several minutes, as if thinking, "Yes, this is interesting, but what's the point?" Our winner's head bobbed and bounced as he kept his grip on the wheel and his forward glare. The car stopped for a few seconds, then resumed the hill-climbing routine, ending in a steep, bumpy descent. The metal claw leveled the car and raised it several more feet, and then, like a last cruel joke, sent it into a wobbly spin, rolling four times before coming to a clanking, hissing rest.

For a moment, the winner broke character: mouth open, wide-eyed, he looked out his side window. Then he faced forward again. The Frenchman, knowing the routine's timing, emerged from the bar scratching his beard. He put his beer bottle on the platform before climbing back on. He went straight to the little box, pushed the lever up, and opened the car door to unstrap the young man, who stepped out steadily, to my surprise, and put on his bored look as he rejoined the crowd. The young man ignored the Frenchman, who ignored him. That was the "Rothman's Rally."

The spectacle was in town for three days to promote Rothman's sponsorship of the Paris-Dakar Rally scheduled in March. The race—billed as a contest of man against his environment—would cross the Sahara through Morocco and Mauritania to Dakar. Dozens of souped-up cars and motorcycles with support vehicles and aircraft would streak across desert and savanna, through villages and farm fields (as racers had done in many rallies before in Niger and Mali), maiming or killing the occasional farm animal, and sometimes the unwary person. A fist in the face from Europe, like an invited guest who casually wrecks the house.

I got lost one afternoon in Zinder looking for the offices of the regional medical officer, who had information about road accidents. I ended up wandering through ruins on the city's edge, building after crumbling building the French colonizers had built for themselves. I decided to keep wandering—through offices, barracks, armories, and handsome stone homes dating back to the beginning of the colony in 1900, when Zinder was the colonial capital.

The French had occupied a hilltop in the eastern section of the city, up the road from the Hotel Central and the *bureau de poste* and past the Musée *Regionale*. This is the same road that joins Route 1 as it heads out of the city and runs east another 375 miles to Lake Chad. Forced labor crews had plastered the buildings with white stucco over mud bricks six inches thick. The stucco, now yellowed, was flaking off under the erosive forces of rain and wind. Triangular decorative battlements, like teeth, concealed corrugated iron roofs. Many of the roofs and walls had collapsed. The remaining structures looked like dried-out broken eggs tossed aside, the yoke left to rot.

People once entered these buildings up wide stairs, across broad patios, and through high archways flanked by six-foot French windows. I entered the buildings by stepping over the remains of a wall or through a window opening.

Time had erased the more human traces of the French in these places. No furniture or shelving remained, not even a rusting bed frame; no papers, bits of photographs, clothing, wall hangings, or cookware—nothing to connect me personally to people who lived and worked in these buildings on a hilltop thirty-two years before. I found only vague random clues: bits of pipe, pieces of a white commode bolted to the floor, a chunk of a sink, electrical wiring, sections of checkered black-and-white floor tiles.

The structures, by design, demanded attention and created a military advantage. From this summit the French once administered a system that forced villagers to surrender quotas of cotton and peanuts for export, young men for colonial military service, and huge labor crews to build roads all across Niger. Elders in Zinder told me that hundreds died building Route 1 and other roads, but the French kept no records of casualties. Men, women, and children worked in teams, the women and young ones hauling buckets of laterite rock from the bush while the men pounded and graded the material into the road. French engineers surveyed the work on horseback and kept crews under the armed watch of colonial military conscripts from Mali and Senegal. The French paid the workers a few francs a day and required village chiefs to provide food and water without compensation. This hardship, the French insisted, was for the common good, for the betterment of the region. The crews slept where they worked, and people died of thirst, starvation, and disease. Beatings were routine for those who lagged behind. Some were shot. None of this can be verified through the records the French left behind. Why, after all, would they incriminate themselves? I had only the word of the very old in Zinder.

The French did more than draft labor crews. That much is well documented. Young men from villages with names like Gouré, Magaria, Droum, and Mirria were made to put on French uniforms and taken to die in incomprehensible wars defined in Paris, Berlin, London, and Brussels, their bodies fallen in places like Verdun and Dien Bien Phu—all for the glory of France.

Zinder's regional archive, a small building behind the governor's office (Zinder is now the capital of one of Niger's seven regional departments), holds great volumes of decaying official history. Inside, on wooden shelves and in a pyramid pile on the floor, are reports, letters, orders. I read, in a green cardboard binder, a directive dated June 28, 1916, typed on onionskin under the title "Police des Routes." The commandant in Zinder sent it unsigned, as if in a hurry, to the post commander in Tanout, seventy miles north on the road to Agadez: "Mail convoys are again reporting pillaging by the Mousgous and Kel-Fadey [Tuareg groups]. I have ordered measures be taken to put an end to all hostilities. It is up to you to assure the effective policing of the roads and Tuareg camps."

Now, in the buildings where the colonizers had once lived and worked, the cracking cement and tile floors were strewn with shit. Walking through one stone building, I imagined a Frenchman in white uniform at his desk calculating the cotton harvest, considering the discipline of a village chief, but oblivious to an African dressed in a white coat and standing in a corner, pumping a large bellows to cool him.

The ruins serve a purpose similar to the war ruins deliberately left unrepaired in Europe and Japan. They remind us of something awful. But these ruins mock through negligence, a gesture of contempt through decay.

The French have ceased to matter in this place. The culture of the colonizer has undergone a visual metamorphosis, like the remains of a heavy snow shoveled to one side and left to melt. It is preserved, isolated, only in the cities, such as Niamey, where French, spoken by less than 2 percent of Niger's population, is more commonly heard.

In February 1944, Charles de Gaulle, on a tour of the French African colonies not controlled by the Nazi puppet regime in Vichy, stepped off a twin-engine military transport plane at a dirt airstrip just outside Zinder.[2] The French community of about forty people, joined by groups of African schoolchildren, dignitaries, and colonial soldiers, cheered him down the gangway. The Africans were mostly non-French-speakers dressed traditionally and ordered to be present—village chiefs, provincial sultans, imams, musicians. African civil servants, clerks and teachers assigned to Zinder from France's colonies all over Africa, also attended. They were the only Africans who understood French.

De Gaulle shook hands and complimented the people on their Frenchness, reminding them of the greatness of France, the benevolence of France, assuring them that France would soon end the terrible war—victorious, of course. Minutes later, he walked back up the steps to his plane and flew away, like a man who had quickly understood that he had landed in the wrong place. All along Route 1, the French governed in this absentminded way, neglect punctuated by bursts of fury and paranoia, as if they realized a mistake and didn't want to spend too much energy governing, but couldn't quite make up their minds how to do it. Government by fits and starts.

Not all the colonial buildings have crumbled. A couple of old barracks still house soldiers. A primary school holds classes within the walls of the former French hospital. And the dominant power symbol visible around the city—a rectangular crenellated mud tower built atop a large outcropping of rounded rocks (Zinder's highest point)—marks the headquarters of the regional military garrison (once the French garrison). The garrison includes several hundred men of the regular army and the Garde Republicaine, which provides security for government buildings. They have a single light tank donated by the French.

As I wandered through yet another building, I became aware, suddenly, of two little boys, maybe eight years old, in dust-stained T-shirts and shorts. They stood outside on the patio, staring at me. "*C'est la toilette, Monsieur,*" the taller boy said, not with mockery, but seriously, with the tone of someone who wanted to clear up a slight misunderstanding. They looked at me with faces like empty pages, then hurried away.

I became confused one day when Issoufou Garba called me "Bodo." We were streaking down Route 1 from Maradi to Zinder in the dark when he looked at me, making notes in the passenger seat, keeping my eyes off the road, my mind off the speed. He threw several frowning glances my way, glances he stole from the road, as if he had just noticed something for the first time. He took in my notebook and pen. I was aware of this but did not look back at him.

Issoufou said: "*Toi, tu es Bodo.*"

"*Quoi?*"

"*Tu es Bodo, grand Bodo.*"

Puzzled, I just looked at him. "I don't understand," I said.

"Bodo was a Frenchman," he explained. "He lived here once and worked very hard. Now, when we see someone like that, we call him 'Bodo.' It's part of our language. You should know about him. He helped build the roads."

Memories linger. Bodo is the Hausa storytellers' name for Jean Boudot, a French district officer who long ago entered Zinder legend and lexicon. His personality is the subject of story and song in Niger, and Bodo is a complimentary nickname for those who work very hard. "*Lui là, c'est un grand Bodo,*" people on the street respectfully say of a farmer marching to his fields.

I found that the story still lived in the head of one of Niger's most famous cultural figures, Mazo dan Alalo, the *griot*, or personal praise singer, of every sultan of Zinder since 1940. Mazo told me about Boudot while sitting in an old lawn chair in the sandy compound of his Zinder home, a whitewashed mud mansion built by his father, who had also been a *griot*. Mazo and the elders of Zinder remember the Frenchman with ironic affection and by the title Mazo gave him: Anasara Bodo Sarkin Ayki, "The Christian Boudot, Prince of

Work." They remember him for his management of the forced labor crews who worked the roads and fields and built many of the colonial buildings in Niger. Forced labor built France's colonies the world over. Forced labor built Route 1.

Mazo dan Alalo was in his mid-nineties when I spoke with him (he was not sure of his exact age). He stood six feet tall. The day I met him he was exquisitely robed in bright cotton, white and blue, with tan leather slippers and a thick white turban wound high above his head. His face looked like a scarred fingerprint, marked by wrinkle patterns of crazy slits and lines that converged to center on his nose and mouth. Mazo sang for Boudot, sang about him and against him—that nervous, lanky commandant in white shorts and open-collared shirt, thick shock of coal black hair, explosive temper. "*Un homme toujours faché*"—An always angry man—so Zinder residents still describe him. Boudot had a way of bursting from his office to yell, no matter the occasion, at the nearest person, European or African, man, woman, or child: "*C'est quoi, ça? Tu n'as rien a faire? Pas de travail?*"—What's this? You've nothing to do? No work?

Jean Boudot was *commandant de cercle*—district commandant—of Zinder for only eleven months in 1943 and 1944. His name survives as a metaphor for work. He is also remembered for his peculiar harshness, though he had decades of competition. There was Lieutenant Colombani, for instance, who, in 1925, reportedly kicked a village chief to death on Route 1, just two and a half miles from Zinder. The chief had failed to raise the labor requested for road repairs, and he was too old to rise from his straw mat when the lieutenant stood before him demanding an explanation. Colombani, Mazo and other elders told me, screamed at the chief: "I'll teach you respect!" He kicked the chief off his mat, and kicked again repeatedly at the old man's abdomen. The chief bled to death internally right there on the road. The colonial records reveal nothing of the incident, though the lieutenant's work progress reports survive.

Curiously, few remember Colombani, but everyone knows of Boudot, whose image survives thanks to the *griot*. Schoolchildren learn the Boudot story from the words of Mazo's songs. On loan from the sultan of Zinder, Mazo toured the countryside on horseback with the Frenchman, singing his praises—"Bodo, the friend of the sultan / All the chiefs know his work"—or the praises of his programs, always in Hausa (Mazo still speaks no French, and I interviewed him through an interpreter). Mazo rode his horse right behind the commandant, beating a drum and singing with a half dozen men backing him up, on foot, with voices and drums. They sang as Boudot and his colonial soldiers marched men and women and children out of villages at gunpoint to serve on labor crews, as Boudot ordered a man beaten for taking a rest from his job crushing laterite on the road, as he handed a cash reward—five francs—to a man whose work pleased him. Mazo sang on. He had no choice, really. His situation was similar to that of a regional balladeer conscripted by a state governor to campaign for him in melody.

Bodo Anasara Sarkin Ayki
He who forced us to plant manioc and peanuts
He who forced us to make the roads
Bodo, the son of nonbelievers
The friend of the Sultan

Sarkin Bodo Anasara Sarkin Ayki
He freed no one from work
Who but Bodo would make the old
the lepers, the blind, the prostitutes
the soldiers and their wives do work
Even the marabouts and the roosters
who wake us for prayer went to work

Anasara Bodo Sarkin Ayki . . .[3]

The *griot* as African institution is much more than singer and storyteller. He is also historian and journalist. Mazo was the sultan's unofficial adviser on matters of state, culture, society. He was a listener and reporter of sorts who took the country's social and political pulse. To his sultan, Mazo was spin doctor, ad man, image maker, intelligence gatherer. Spy.

Boudot fell ill often, Mazo told me—stomach problems or malaria. Yet the Frenchman insisted on daily project inspections and personally visited villages to raise work crews. "He would look at a man's hands," Mazo told me, "and if they didn't show the wear of work, Bodo would take him for labor. Sometimes he would beat the man. Bodo had no consideration." Then Mazo added, borrowing a line from his own song, "For Bodo, everything was work."

Subversion permeates Mazo's work, which music dealers sell on cassettes all around Niger. There are many versions of the Bodo song, all Mazo's recordings: he modifies the story as he sings. The listener hears Mazo telling the sultan what he saw and heard, and, in the commandant's very presence, forming a musical caricature to please the sultan, to manipulate villagers' hearts and minds, the balance of power—"Bodo who sends the roosters and lepers to work"; and this variation: "Bodo, who makes even the sultan work." The sultan, of course, never did physical labor. Mazo sang his signature into a story with words that mocked but went right past the ears of the unwary white man who spoke no Hausa. "Who but Bodo would make the old, the lepers, the blind go to work."

Zinder's Birni quarter—the city's oldest neighborhood—is built among clusters of huge rounded rocks that sprout from the flat, sandy landscape, seeming to grow out of one another like cauliflower. The rocks once made useful fortifications and still make good natural walls for houses. Many believe their size indicates the presence of significant power within.

One morning in the summer of 1911 (the year is approximate), two small boys, one Hausa and the other Arab, were playing on a rock the size of a school bus but shaped like the sloping narrow tail of a prehistoric beast. The rock conveniently intruded into the home compound of the Hausa boy, Mahamane dan Chalaga, whose father managed the sultan's vast horse stables. With a little sand tossed on the surface, the rock made a good slide for straw mats.

Mahamane and Hamed Charif, son of a wealthy Arab merchant, chased each other up and down that rock. They tumbled down together and landed in a pile at the bottom, laughing. The rains had been good that summer, and the air was cool after months of heavy, stubborn dry-season heat.

For a few moments, Mahamane sat still in the sand below the great stone. He frowned, not frightened, but listening hard. "Hamed," he said. "Do you hear that?"

A distant ʒʒʒʒʒʒʒ, interrupted by clanking, and then that low ʒʒʒʒʒʒʒ again, unlike any sound they knew. They ran from the compound to investigate, and a short distance down a narrow alleyway almost collided with the thing they had heard—a parked car, driverless, with its motor idling. "When I first saw the car," Mahamane (now in his nineties) told me, "it was alone outside the house of Hamed's family. No one was in it, and it was vibrating all alone, shaking as if it were angry like a beast." I smiled at the fact that these two boys nearly ran over the first car they ever saw, rather than the other way around. "Hamed and I ran back to my family's compound to find my father. We thought we had done something wrong and that the thing was looking for us. We didn't understand what it was." The car's owner, in fact, was Hamed's father, the cloth merchant Charif Dodo.

Zinder is full of road tales, old stories of death and daring on cross-desert trade routes, and the occasional bizarre anecdote, like Mahamane's story of the car he saw as a boy. That machine must have been one of the first automobiles to enter Niger, arriving in the years just before World War I. Mahamane, who was born between

1900 and 1905, told me he was around eleven or twelve years old when he saw the car; he couldn't remember precisely. By 1912, cars were becoming more common in colonial port cities along the West African coast, but they hadn't yet rolled into the interior in noticeable numbers. The French supplied outposts like Zinder by camel and donkey caravans.

The story's details have to be carefully mined from the very old, then sifted and cross-checked. Pieces of hard fact occasionally emerge. Still, nothing is certain. In Zinder, I sought the counsel of the very old, anyone who might have a bit of information. Mazo dan Alalo first mentioned the car to me, but said his memory of it was very poor. He told me about Mahamane and instructed me to look for him at the Sultanate, where many of the city's eldest men and women collect in the morning shade of the high brown walls. I found Mahamane sitting alone on a straw mat with a cane resting across his legs. He was chewing kola nut and fingering prayer beads while clutching a camelhair blanket about him against the cold-season air. Like his father before him, Mahamane had been the caretaker of the sultan's horses—only a dozen now, though they had numbered more than a thousand during his father's time.

That car, Mahamane and others told me (people whose parents and grandparents had seen it), could carry four passengers: the driver and one more up front, two in back. It was an American car, Mahamane and Mazo insisted, which Charif had bought in Kano, British Nigeria, eighty miles to the south. In the absence of roads, he arranged for it to be towed through the bush to Zinder by a pair of camels, a week's journey.

Most likely the car was a Ford, probably a Model T, which Ford introduced in 1908 and followed up with variations, including one that completed the 1912 Peking-to-Paris Rally. The Model T became one of the most widely driven cars in the world before World War I; fifteen million were sold before Ford switched to the Model A in 1928.

What the people saw in Zinder resembled a horseless buggy with thin, airless rubber tires that stuck easily in sand. An impractical machine in the Sahel, but an important symbol of wealth.

Mahamane, as far as I could tell, was the only surviving witness with a clear memory of what may have been Niger's first automobile the very day it arrived in Zinder. Such a bizarre object, a thing so otherworldly in a city that for centuries had depended on the trade of camel caravans, could not have been a secret for any amount of time. Mahamane and Hamed ran through the city to spread the news of the "shaking beast."

The morning I met Mahamane, we walked to his home, the very same house where he grew up. He showed me the great rock. Mahamane walked with his cane, taking long, slow strides, carefully placing the tip with every step, his body stooped under his blanket. "It was many days," he told me, standing again at the foot of the rock, "before Hamed and I had the courage to touch that car without running away." But he could not remember the year he saw the vehicle. "Was it around 1912?" I asked. He shrugged.

Mahamane showed me, too, where Charif Dodo and his family had lived. The house was a ruin. The skeleton of a Peugeot sedan lay crumpled and half buried within waist-high mud walls that were melting steadily under wind and rain. The car's front half protruded like a tombstone, facing the street as if glaring at passersby. The family had faded into rumor ("They all died" or "They returned to Algeria"). Not even Mahamane recalled. Only the memory of the car, perhaps the most remarkable thing about Charif Dodo, remained.

Charif, who had the money to risk eccentricity, bought bundles of dried grass and millet stalks and hired men to lay a mile or so of track around the city. Thus, Niger's first functional motor roads were dual platforms of tightly bound and flattened grass bundles, spliced end to end along the routes Charif wanted to drive—to the Sultanate, the homes of friends, his shops, the colonial offices. The French and the sultan, always jealous and suspicious of one another's influence, had no motor vehicles of their own. The French commandant is said to have borrowed the car for tours of the city and for road inspections.

It is a point of no small significance that an Arab, a member of a group who for hundreds of years were the masters of cross-Saharan trade, was possibly the first to own a car and build motor roads in Niger. Although the French had established a wagon and caravan route along what is now Route 1, they did not yet maintain it for automobiles.

Mahamane spoke skeptically of the automobile he saw as a boy. "What good was it?" he said. "They couldn't take the thing out in the bush." When I met him, he still preferred to walk. Mahamane had been in a car only a half dozen times in his life.

The French soon brought in their own cars and began building more roads and, during the late 1920s, the Zinder airstrip. Charif Dodo eventually sold his car, people say, and what happened to it after that is anybody's guess. I like to think the machine is still around in spirit and substance, scattered about West Africa in pieces, some of them still on the road. A spring fitted in one vehicle somewhere, a bolt that proved useful in another somewhere else; or perhaps a chunk of sheet metal from its body shades a family's doorway.

One afternoon around Christmas 1987 (near the end of my Peace Corps service), on Zinder's windswept streets near the *bureau de poste*, a large, snub-nosed truck with a gray cab rumbled past me. The truck was Nigerian, what they call a mammy wagon, with high wooden walls around the rear bed, like a big box, and painted in many colors. I recall pictures of lions, men in battle with big guns, and an English slogan, "GOD SAVE US!"

What had caught my attention, however, was something painted long before on the driver's-side door—a German Army cross, thick black and trimmed on the outside edges with thin white borders. Only a shadow of the cross remained. Just enough. The truck was moving slowly enough that I could run back and verify that the trademark sign on the radiator grille said Ford, not Mercedes, and that the door was a darker shade of gray than the rest of the body. It was a modified truck, and not unusual, except for the door and its insignia, whose origins fascinated me. A stray fragment, perhaps, of Rommel's Afrika Corps, which fought the British on the other side of the Sahara; a door rescued from shreds of hardware blown to bits in a tank battle between machines painted the color of sand, fighting in white heat like scorpions; or perhaps a door from a truck captured and sold, whole or piece by piece, at the war's end.

The memory returned in February 1993 when I was walking through Zinder's open market, in the section known as Kasuan Tsakuwa—the metal market. Metalsmiths, dozens of them spread over two acres, working with scrap metal or, literally, road metal, bits of metal from everywhere, but primarily the road. They reshape metal pieces into bed frames, cooking utensils, plates, bowls, axes, hoes, plow blades, nails and hammers, screws and screwdrivers, hinges, doors, roofing, tables, chairs, daggers and swords, tea trays, cooking stoves, travel chests, bicycle frames, eyeglasses, and back into car parts such as doors and engine hoods. And from tires and inner tubes they make sandals, shoe soles, rubber hoses, watch straps, saddlebags, and well buckets.

A playground of ingenuity, genius born of need.

The material comes from car wrecks, from parts hunted and plucked carefully like wild mushrooms, judged for value and carried to market alongside vegetables and grains, part of the general national harvest. A station wagon may kill seven passengers, but in death it preserves the livelihood of a family or two from the closest village—the first to arrive at the scene after the bodies have been cleared away and the gendarmes have finished their note-taking. It could happen no other way.

In Africa, everything is adaptable. Old bicycle frames, oil barrels from Nigeria, cans, corrugated iron, and automobile scraps such as car bodies or a heavy steel chassis too mangled to be repaired. The metal market assumes the character of a slaughterhouse, where nothing is wasted and from which everything emerges with a new identity, like cuts of meat so neatly, antiseptically packaged for the supermarket. The metalsmiths buy the raw metal; the salvageable engine parts go to mechanics and parts dealers.

The smiths handle Western technology a little like instant coffee, if you stretch the image. Their working material is soluble, filtered through mutilation, reshaped, redefined, reborn, redistributed, and redigested again and again and again. Nothing, perhaps, is quite what it seems or was intended to be. It is simple; it is African, a question of ingenuity and survival. You use what you have, what you can find.

The road, the aged road
Retched on this fresh plunder
Of my youth.
— Wole Soyinka, "In Memory of Segun Awolowo"

Driving to Madness

here he is," Issoufou Garba said, gazing out the car windshield into gritty haze. "There's my little imbecile. Do you see him?"

"*Non,*" I said. I didn't see him, the man Issoufou called "*mon petit imbécile.*" For some reason the words seem clearer now in the original French, as if my memory of the man we sought is frozen in the phonetics. An ice cube of thought. In French, the syllables of *imbécile* bounce louder from the lips, and they can be drawn out, emphasized with a sharp kick of the tongue at the end. *Iimmbéecciila.* Which was what Issoufou was doing, drawling the word to himself as he watched the man I couldn't see—a *komasho.* Issoufou's own.

I looked out the window again. "Where is he?" I squinted and leaned over on the seat, looking past Issoufou.

He frowned at me, a little impatient, and pointed once more, casually flicking his left hand behind him with the index finger out, the way one might point out the village idiot. "*Tu vois? C'est lui, là.*" Issoufou laughed just a little, nodding his head slightly, suggesting he had made eye contact with this person. He turned off the engine.

We were sitting in Issoufou's Peugeot station wagon, on a road just outside the crowded motor park in Maradi, a market city near the border with Nigeria. Two vast fields separated by a long, low cement wall in the center make up the motor park. As a border town, Maradi is economically more complex, bigger, dirtier, wealthier, more dangerous than Niger's other cities. An African Tijuana. You can buy anything in Maradi: Snickers bars, grains and vegetables, genuine or fake designer jeans, baseball gloves (no one plays in Niger), automatic arms, smuggled gasoline. The stuff comes up from Nigeria, that African catchall economic Goliath.

In the street, dense streams of people—women and girls balancing pots of rice and beans atop their heads, people on market business, people with no business, children, travelers, idlers—drifted and collected, moving this way and that, congealing at shops, in the shade of trees, at street-side coffee tables where rows of men—only men—sat and talked. Women in small groups walked by on errands or stood to chat for a few minutes as they passed one another on the street. One woman sat at a cooking fire frying millet flour cakes in peanut oil. She wrapped them by the dozen in newspaper and sold them to passersby. Only men seemed to lounge with nothing to do. The street was so crowded, the din of voices and engines and animals so constant, that I couldn't tell whom Issoufou was pointing at.

When we reached Maradi early that morning, the gendarmes at the city entrance hadn't bothered with us. I didn't know why. As we arrived at the checkpoint, a soldier, clutching himself against the cool February Harmattan winds, simply lowered the rope and waved us on. Four other soldiers were huddled around the driver of an eighteen-wheeler. Bigger prey, maybe.

Around 1:00 P.M. we found ourselves back among the *komasho*, a dozen young men and boys who right away saw we were looking for someone. Issoufou was pointing. The *komasho* closed in. They pounded on the windows, they thumped the roof, they shouted.

"Monsieur Issouf, c'est moi! Tu me connais, tu me connais, c'est moi!"—
It's me, you know me, you know me, it's me!

Now, just ahead of us, I saw a man who looked a little evil. It was,
I suppose, his face. He coasted briskly along my side of the car at the
head of a group of four men, like pirates preparing to board and loot.
The evil one, the leader, was short, overly muscular, slightly stooped,
frowning from a lumpy face, like a troll. A Maradi *komasho*.

His name was Abdou, and he was one of Issoufou's contacts. I
had never met him before, but I knew enough to be careful. Judging
by his appearance, his strength, the newness of his clothing, he did
better than most *komasho*. He stood there with his face in my window, grinning and rapping his knuckles softly on the glass. He didn't
have to shout.

Abdou wore a heavy, ill-fitting brown canvas suit, homespun and
new. His sandals were blue plastic, a cheap Chinese import. He had
shaved his head, and his face was smooth skinned, lean, and square.
The prominent nose and chin combined with high cheekbones and
jutting forehead to make his visage appear lumpy, like a big potato.
Thick tendons like lengths of bark ran up his forearms. His sunglasses were a style normally worn by women, the top-heavy plastic kind with bows attached to the bottom of wide oval lens frames.
The inside seams of Abdou's trousers wiggled out of control down
his thighs, and the cuffs were uneven by an inch. Issoufou's contempt,
his use of the French-English cognate *imbécile,* and that nervous
chuckle came to my mind. But I didn't feel like laughing.

Too risky.

All at once, Issoufou leaned over and thrust an arm behind my
seat to unlock the rear door. Abdou yanked it open immediately. He
slid in the backseat and slammed and locked the door against his
competitors, who orbited the car, arguing amongst themselves. They
peered at us through the windows, some frowning and others wav-

ing and smiling at me while the troll sat behind Issoufou and leaned forward to clamp his right hand on my friend's shoulder, still grinning. The grin's persistence carried a psychopathic quality, emphasizing that the hand-on-shoulder was not a gesture of friendship but a reminder of the strength of the hand's owner.

One of the men outside the car put his ear to my window; another did the same on the driver's side. But Issoufou and Abdou ignored all this. They dispensed with greetings, going straight to business while Issoufou simultaneously studied the streets, in case one of Abdou's more earnest competitors should decide to challenge Abdou more pointedly. The *komasho* did this occasionally to destroy one another's business contacts.

"I've got two, Issoufou," Abdou said hoarsely, just above a whisper, aware of the ears outside. He ignored me. I was just another white traveler to him—a tourist? a missionary? a Peace Corps volunteer? It didn't matter. I was Issoufou's own merchandise, a nonissue. Already sold freight.

The man at my window pressed his lips against the glass, then his tongue, laying it flat against the surface like a pink snail. He backed off a moment, laughing, watching for my reaction. I watched him blankly as he prodded me with a wide toothy smile, raising his eyebrows repeatedly. Another man sat calmly on the hood, hunched over in the shape of a gargoyle, his chin on his knees and his legs crossed at the ankles. Others circled the car. I folded my arms across my chest, a gesture of defense, of digging in.

Abdou and Issoufou continued talking in low tones. I heard Abdou say: "They weren't easy to find, Issouf. This will cost you."

I remember the actions of many *komasho* in Niger, and in Nigeria and Ivory Coast and Senegal: their bobbing, swirling, biting presence, but not what they all looked like. The details mix in my head: bare feet, sores, ragged dust-stained clothes, mostly trousers and

American T-shirts. No faces. This is important: The man at my window suddenly grabbed his shirttail, vigorously wiped the smoky smear of his saliva from the glass where his tongue had been, and walked away. As if he were suddenly sorry. Another man took his place, kneeling at the window to look at me. This man wore a T-shirt, dirty white, with "FOREST RANGERS DO IT IN TREES" in large green block letters on the front.

Issoufou asked: "Where are my passengers?" He looked at Abdou in his rearview mirror and smiled broadly, trying to match the *komasho*'s persistent grin and keep the tone calm and easy.

Abdou leaned forward, unimpressed, his hand still heavy on Issoufou's shoulder. He drilled a glare and an order into Issoufou's ear. "They are coming, Issouf." He slapped the top of the seat. Issoufou looked at him for a moment, and then over at me. Issoufou smiled. "We wait," he said.

Niger has a highway police unit, the Brigade Routière, a part of the Gendarmerie Nationale. Speed limit signs are posted, but Niger's open roads are unpatrolled, and drivers unmonitored for their attention to speed and traffic laws. This is true in most African countries. Governments don't have the resources to support full-fledged highway patrols. In Niger, there are only ragtag bands of men at checkpoints, wearing old fatigues and the green berets of gendarmes. The Brigade Routière.

In a motor park garage, just a parcel of open ground under a tree, I once watched a gendarme sergeant bring in his personal car to have the fuel filter changed, and later drive away without paying, leaving only this promise: "I'll find you if my car breaks down."

In Niamey, I went one day to meet the brigade commandant, but an aide outside his office told me I would have to get permission first. He didn't know where I could obtain such permission. For weeks I was passed down a line of *gendarmerie* and army officers ("I'm sorry, I don't have the authority to talk to you," I was told. "Go see Lieutenant So-and-so"), and bounced back and forth between ministries (Defense, Transport, Interior).

One Friday afternoon, after spending a day working my way up three floors of the Gendarmerie Nationale, where I had become a minor fixture ("Ah, it's you again. Haven't you found the commandant?"), I was standing in a small room with a lieutenant, a man named Idrissa. He was tall and thin and serious, his head clean-shaven, and he wore a dress khaki tunic and trousers, and polished black leather shoes. The room had a desk and chair, and Lieutenant Idrissa received me without offering his hand or asking me to sit. I was being interrogated, albeit halfheartedly. We spoke in French.

"What is your research?"

"I'm writing about road transport."

"Why? What is so special about Niger?"

I tried to be cheerful, personable, standing with my hands folded politely in front of me. "You are said to have the best road system in West Africa," I explained. In fact, Niger's roads, built with profits from its Saharan uranium mines, are among West Africa's best. "Maybe there is something to be learned from Niger's experience."

He frowned, shook his head. "I doubt it." Then, "Do you have a research authorization?" I smiled, though uneasy, and handed him a copy of the document, which had the minister of education's signature. He put the paper on his desk after a glance and looked back at me. "Have you ever been in the military?"

"No." I added a hopeful detail: "I was in the Peace Corps, here in Niger." This did not soften him. He did not seem to hear me. Then he said, "I'll keep your authorization." (It was only a copy.) "The commandant will see you Monday morning at eight. And he'll want to see a list of your questions before he talks with you."

I wondered whether this meeting had been just a formality,

that they didn't know what else to do with me except give me the interview.

It was 4:00 P.M. Issoufou had stopped the Peugeot at a small mosque on the edge of Gazaoua, a village that straddles Route 1. He wanted to pray because he had missed the midday prayer. The mud brick buildings spread and then quickly faded out over a thinly forested plain 50 miles east of the city of Maradi, 7 miles north of Nigeria, and 360 miles south of Algeria.

As it turned out, Abdou did have the passengers he had promised—four men who had been waiting for us at a coffee table a few hundred yards down the street. After thirty minutes, Abdou brought them, each carrying a nylon or plastic handbag. Another half hour passed as he and Issoufou, standing beside the car, argued over price. The other *komasho* had wandered away in search of new opportunities. Abdou would lean forward into Issoufou's face—"Issouf, I could have sold them to someone else"—while Issoufou stood, arms folded, calmly toeing the dirt, smiling and waiting. Finally, Issoufou paid him twenty-five hundred CFA francs—five hundred francs more than Issoufou had first offered, and five hundred francs less than what Abdou had first demanded—and we started back to Zinder on an afternoon so windy and hazy that it almost appeared to be snowing.

Now, in Gazaoua, I was standing while the others prayed, on the road, watching sand blow over my boots. I was wearing a gray cotton turban that protected my face and mouth. The sand moving below my knees was different from the haze that hung around me: a dust storm, fine, gritty fog, light and dense, lifted high in the atmosphere by steady winds.

Sand washed around my ankles, blowing southwest in gentle brown streams and creating the illusion that the earth's surface had softened to the texture of cotton. A sandstorm requires meaner winds, twenty miles per hour or more, to move heavier particles in low sheets, usually no higher than chest level. The sandstorms of the West African Sahel look sometimes like thin creeks and at other times like broad rivers of hissing sand. These storms are not all benign. Sandstorms can quickly build deep drifts and small dunes. They occasionally bury stranded cars, even abandoned villages. The storm at my feet, though, moved mildly.

Issoufou, religious and conscientious, liked to stop in Gazaoua, a few miles west of a government checkpoint at the town of Tessaoua. We stopped there on every return trip, sometimes to pray or to find food and water. And now, watching him finish his prayers, a kerchief tied around his face from the nose down, it occurred to me that Issoufou had made this stop to prepare himself. The Tessaoua gendarmes harassed Zinder drivers only on their way home from Maradi—when they knew drivers had more money to give up. Issoufou won his battles through quiet stubbornness—that folded-arms-toeing-the-dirt pose he seemed able to hold indefinitely. He swore the gendarmes at Tessaoua hated bush taxi drivers, resented their freedom and the money they made. Issoufou rarely revealed nervousness, but I saw it that afternoon as he repeatedly dried his hands on the breast of his blue cotton tunic.

A rumor I'd heard many times in the motor parks claimed that the Tessaoua soldiers had in the past year beaten to death a bush taxi driver who was making the trip east from Niamey at night. I could never confirm the story. Yet the rumor survived among the drivers, fed by fresh details of other offenses, a sort of indirect evidence.

I collected my own such corroboration. I once saw a soldier inexplicably beat a young man at one checkpoint, and at many others I watched soldiers yank people off vehicles for reasons never made clear. On several occasions I saw drivers beaten for not having "proper registration papers." On a trip we took a month before this one, the Tessaoua gendarmes kept Issoufou's car documents for two hours without explanation. They took all the passengers' papers, including my passport. The gendarmes ignored Issoufou's inquiries and asked nothing. As we waited, they sat and played cards beside the documents, which they had stacked on a bench.

A simple demonstration of power.

After the gendarmes gave back our papers, Issoufou returned to the car in quiet rage that barely broke the crust of his personality. He spit his words as he started the engine. "Those soldiers, without these roads they would have nothing to do. Nothing!"

When I first began traveling with Issoufou, he made me promise that I was not a CIA spy or white mercenary. He didn't want additional problems with gendarmes. I laughed at this. "Issoufou, what could I possibly be spying on around here?" He merely looked at me, not seeing the humor. I gave him my word, but for some weeks he kept me at a distance when we were on the road. In the presence of other passengers or drivers, it was difficult to talk with him, especially to discuss his work or ask questions.

Niger has little experience with mercenaries, but conspiracy theories are popular. There are many authentic examples of white mercenaries—opportunists and French Foreign Legionnaires—bringing down or manipulating African governments. In 1979, French soldiers managed the overthrow of Emperor Bokassa in the Central African Republic. They have intervened in Chad and Gabon, and thousands are based in the Ivory Coast and Senegal. Bob Denard, the French mercenary and former Legionnaire who twice took power and named himself head of the government of the Comoros Islands, is legendary in Africa. In Niger, every stranger, every white person, is a suspect agent of the American CIA or the French Sûreté. Everyone blames the Tuareg rebellion on French treachery. Once, a passenger in Issoufou's car told me he was sure the Sahel's persistent drought and the advancing Sahara Desert were the work of some high-tech French effort to control its former colonies. Passengers who saw my notebook and heard my questions ("Issoufou, how much do you spend on car repairs every week?") glared at me.

"Who are you?" a passenger asked me one day. "Why do you ask so many questions? Are you CIA? Are you working for the rebellion?"

Later that same day, Issoufou told me: "You have to be careful of what you say and what you ask in this country." I felt ashamed of my naiveté. I learned to shut up. The more I traveled in Niger, the more it became obvious that the ubiquitous checkpoints did not serve the purpose of extortion alone, but also satisfied a paranoid fear of strangers, of anything foreign, in a country divided by eight languages and ethnic groups. Separated from each other by language, the people of Niger live in a continuous state of mutual distrust and jealousy. There was also the very real security threat posed by the Tuareg rebels.

Almost weekly there were new motor park rumors and radio reports of rebel ambushes. On a remote road in a village called Keita, hundreds of miles northwest of Zinder, rebels seized several vehicles from a development project. A petrol tanker was blown up on Route 2 near Agadez, and another was seized on the road from Zinder to Agadez. Clashes between soldiers and rebels were routine in the desert north of Agadez, but when rebels began hitting farther south in the area around Zinder, the paranoia got worse. Rebels attacked a bush taxi fleet near a rural marketplace one hundred miles north of Zinder and ambushed the army patrol sent to hunt them down. One soldier was killed and another wounded. That same day, rebels shot to death a village chief in that area. People speculated that a big attack was planned on Route 1 or on Zinder itself, though it never happened. In fact, I never witnessed a rebel action, though my presence, the possibility that I was a mercenary, was always suspect. Gendarmes took extra time to examine my papers.

Issoufou's uneasiness about me gradually relaxed, though it took a couple of months. I hung around and tried to show my interest unobtrusively, sympathetically. We endured dozens of checkpoint confrontations and spent hours together broken down in the wind and heat, waiting for help from a passing car on some isolated patch of road on our way to Maradi or the smaller towns of Tanout to the north and Gouré to the east. We spent nights in the Maradi motor park, sleeping in the car, doors locked against thieves known to roam the park at night with knives. Once, when we ran out of gas on the way to Gouré (the fuel gauge was broken and Issoufou had miscalculated his reserves), we left the passengers behind and hiked three miles through the bush to a village where he knew gas smugglers he could buy from. Through every mishap and hour of discomfort, Issoufou preserved his calm and optimism, uttering, *"Hakuri, hakuri,"* the Hausa word for "patience," as if to keep himself and me in check. Frustrations that certainly would have broken me in time, he took in his stride. Anger could only add to the clutter.

So the memory of his outrage at the Tessaoua gendarmes—"Those soldiers, without these roads, they would have nothing"—stayed with me, surfacing every time we passed a checkpoint. I thought of it now in Gazaoua, turning to face the car, where Issoufou was folding his prayer rug.

At the rural high school in the village of Bouza, Niger, where I was a Peace Corps English teacher, the headmaster would receive a telegram announcing a Ministry of Education inspection. On the appointed day a deputy minister would come up the dirt road from Route 1 (thirty-six miles south of the village) in a fleet of three Land Rovers, one of them holding a few soldiers. The official would cancel classes and call a staff meeting to explain a vaccination program or a new policy, to discuss test scores, and so on. The soldiers, meanwhile, patrolled the grounds. The minister himself came once, bringing a light tank that crouched outside during the staff meeting. A more powerful means of communication than a memo or fuzzy phone call.

Nigerien bureaucrats are poorly trained and underpaid. Telephones work barely, electricity is unreliable or nonexistent outside regional capitals, and computers are thus impractical. Few see television. Most people have a radio, but its voice is a distant, disembodied, suspect presence.

So there is the road: a manual means to execute policy, provide services, and remind the population of a central authority. Roads are the most consistent evidence of government in Niger. District capitals, of course, straddle important motor roads, which also coincide with secondary schools, major medical services, and most large markets. Primary schools, medical dispensaries, and agricultural services are only thinly sprinkled in bush villages. The government sends officials on *tournée* to collect information, explain policy, and be seen. An imperfect, inefficient method of rule, but workable and cheap in a country where civil servants are perpetually owed five months' back pay and foreign donors provide half the $400 million national budget.

Show of strength is key. Niger's security forces number two thousand, and most of them serve on the roads—at tremendous expense, though the government won't say how much. Official extortion (what diplomats call "informal taxation") helps to pay the soldiers—in Niger and in countries across Africa—and the overall cost to the national economy may be impossible to measure precisely. I'm talking about the money siphoned off at checkpoints. Government and transport union officials in Niger, Mali, and Ivory Coast say the losses to merchants, transporters, and ordinary citizens run in the tens of millions of dollars annually, devastating losses to struggling, underdeveloped countries. A World Bank economist I met in Ivory Coast told me, "The amount of money is certainly dramatic, but to calculate a figure for West Africa would be impossible."[1] In an April 1995 story on West Africa's economic malaise, *New York Times* reporter Howard French described a trip he took between the capitals of Burkina Faso and Ghana: "On one recent 600-mile drive from Ouagadougou to Accra, there were no fewer than 30 police and customs checks. Those who brave the route . . . say they are routinely held up for bribes or forced at each stop to surrender portions of their belongings."[2]

The checkpoint is an African road institution, analogous to the American speed trap, where travelers expect to do battle. On Route 1 there is a checkpoint about every twenty-five miles. Nigerian writer Chinua Achebe's 1987 novel, *Anthills of the Savannah*, climaxes in violence at a checkpoint on a fictional African country's "Great North Road." "Security forces!" the narrative scoffs. "Who or what are they securing?" In that tragic scene, a character named Chris challenges a drunken soldier, who "unslung his gun, cocked it, narrowed his eyes while confused voices went up all around. . . . Chris stood his ground looking straight into the man's face, daring him to shoot. And he did, point blank."[3]

Such scenarios breed easily. In Niger it is a crime to be without a national identity card, a law enforced by checking road travelers. This provides soldiers with endless opportunities for mischief. And it means that the traveler in Niger is always crossing a border and being challenged for the right to pass. The traveler must show papers that link his or her face to an identity, a profession, a country. Identity papers grant the right to be on the road, as if the road were a special place, an exclusive meeting point, like a sort of club, not just for any citizen. The penalty for not producing an identity card is loss of travel rights, jail, and a five-hundred-franc fine, which few can pay. Identity cards provide information for a running census on population size, where people live, what they do, and, most important, which ethnic group they belong to. The information is valuable for organizing services, such as estimating and providing food needs during famine, and for keeping tabs on people.

In the United States, we keep vast data networks for the same purposes: tax and driving records; criminal, bank, telephone, school, social security, birth, automobile, and health records; military draft registrations; credit histories; newspaper subscriptions; library cards. Get stopped for speeding, and in seconds the cop calls up your criminal and driving histories, if any, on a computer attached to the dashboard, or radios someone at the station to do it instead. Apply for an apartment and your credit is immediately available to the landlord.

In Niger, however, the government doesn't know you exist—no one but those in your family, village, or neighborhood do—unless you get snagged at a road checkpoint or need to, say, apply for food aid at a district capital. On a road, of course.

Issoufou kept up an easy pace during the short drive to Tessaoua. We merged into thin dust that quickly became denser than the dust we had seen in Maradi early that morning. It coated my teeth, tongue, gums. I wrapped the turban tighter around my head.

In twenty minutes we were in the market town and district capital of Tessaoua. Mud houses blended with the dust, like a world dipped in dirty skim milk. We rolled easily through the town's empty streets, passing no checkpoint. We slowed to a crawl when we began to emerge on the eastern side of town, near the checkpoint that we knew waited yards ahead. Just a cement guard hut and a crude rope hung low across the road. We were looking for it, hoping we would not overrun the rope and anger the gendarmes.

"The gendarme lives the problems of the road." I was sitting, courtesy of Lieutenant Idrissa, on the appointed Monday morning in the office of Moctar Saley, commandant of the Brigade Routière. He was telling me what I had expected to hear. "The gendarme understands the problems of the road. He is honest and very well trained."

Commandant Saley's office felt like a large closet. He worked in the brigade's one-story cement administration building inside a gendarme training compound in Niamey. There was a small window and a broken electric ceiling fan, and the walls were covered with the narrow brown dribbles of rainy-season roof leaks. Saley sat behind a metal desk empty of paperwork, wearing clean, pressed camouflage fatigues and sandals. He was in his forties, balding, very straight in his chair, trim, startlingly soft-spoken. A career soldier. Behind the desk hung a very bad watercolor portrait of him in khaki uniform poised at that desk with pen in hand, over paperwork.

Everyone I spoke to along the chain of command had handed me some generality about Moctar Saley. Scrupulously honest. A man of impressive reserve and control. A devout Muslim, husband, father of eight. A former Brigade Routière officer in five of Niger's seven regional departments, and now, for the past four years, overall brigade commandant. "Yes, a very good man," said an official of the national drivers' union. "But we think he is not very aware of reality on the road. It is a question of isolation. Commandant Saley has done his time in the field, and now he stays in Niamey."

When I arrived in Saley's office, he was cordial, rising to offer me his hand across the desk. He asked to see a written list of my questions, which I produced. He studied them silently while I waited, watching a boy in ragged shorts and T-shirt sit in the doorway polishing the commandant's boots with spittle and a dirty rag. Saley smiled and handed the list back to me, then leaned forward and clasped his hands atop his desk. He said, "*Bon, alors?*"

I sat in a bare metal chair with my notebook in my lap. "What are the most serious problems you find on Niger's roads," I began softly, testing his responses.

"The national highways are exposed to excessive speed and driver impudence," Saley said, leaning on his elbows, his arms folded, looking straight at me. I listened and made notes. "Many drivers are completely untrained and neglect the mechanical needs of their cars and the safety of their passengers. They collect the fare and drive until their cars fall apart."

Another question: "Are road conditions safer now than when you joined the brigade?"

He shook his head gravely. "The situation is worse. There are more accidents than ever." Saley did not gesture when he spoke, or even alter his tone, as if he felt his words needed no help to be understood. I looked for an opportunity to casually insert a question not on the submitted list but of great interest to me: I wanted to ask him about corruption and lack of discipline in the brigade. Saley continued. "We do not have the resources, the people, and the vehicles to patrol the roads competently."

Saley's answers came like this for half an hour, predictable, narrow, passive, no casual straying from the subject. A lecture. I was becoming restless. I said, "But," and he raised his hand to stop me. When he finished a response, he said, "*Bon, question trois?*" and later, "*Alors, question quatre?*"

"Yes," I said, late in the interview, ignoring the next question on my list, "but why do you think drivers are like this, so seemingly irresponsible, as you put it."

"They are just greedy," he said. "Drivers are not well educated or honest people. They don't take care of their cars."

The statement annoyed me. I thought of mechanics in their open-air "garages" repairing police vehicles under threat, and of the bush taxis that come in for repairs—often pushed in by passengers and the cash-poor driver, who promises the mechanic he will pay what he can when he can.

In Niger, secondhand cars are repaired with parts recycled or refashioned from other parts, over and over again. Mechanics are like battlefield surgeons inadequately trained and rushed to the front. They are few and poorly equipped. They live lives of periodic idleness and frenzy. Curled up asleep on an oily mat one moment, maybe for a whole day, and then suddenly buzzing about prioritizing the wounded, going without rest or food. Sleep and triage. They work with what they have, tools and parts strewn about the oil-stained dirt amid stripped auto carcasses—compact cars and minibuses—scattered here and there, twisted and empty like dried orange rinds.

I looked up from my notes and smiled.

"Yes," I said, "but don't you think there are similar problems of greed and corruption among gendarmes at your checkpoints? You must be aware, commandant, that drivers are always complaining of how gendarmes take money from them at checkpoints, even from passengers, and often without explanation or reason. I've seen this myself. After all, wasn't that one of the main complaints drivers brought up during the strike?" I heard my voice letting the question get out of hand, more to the point than I had planned, breaking the seal of the interview. "I understand there is even an occasional beating."

For a moment Saley stared at me, unblinking, like an actor who had been fed a line not in the script. But he was off balance only for that one moment.

"I have never heard of this happening, and I don't know what you saw," he said. "All behavior found to be unbecoming of a gendarme in the brigade is severely sanctioned. That I can assure you, Monsieur." The last sentence Saley spoke slowly, pausing briefly between each word, and rising to his feet as he finished.

Without looking up from my notebook, pretending not to see him, I asked, "Can you give me an example of when you have disciplined a gendarme?" I looked up only when the commandant did not answer.

He said, "*C'est fini, Monsieur.*"

Issoufou suddenly punched the brakes hard, and we slid on the sandy road, stopping a foot away from the checkpoint rope. I saw it only now. Dust had all but obscured the cement guard hut. A couple of yards off the road a gendarme sat on a wooden bench, hunched over and buried in a woolen military greatcoat, lapels pulled high, arms folded, his face tucked into his chest. An old bolt-action rifle leaned between his legs, the barrel against his folded arms. He lifted a dust-caked khaki face so pale that it looked painted. The gendarme peered at us and jerked his head impatiently at the rope, and buried his face again. I reached inside my shirt to touch the amulet around my neck, to be sure it was there.

Issoufou studied the man for a moment. He pulled his kerchief over his nose against the dust and got out of the car, waving and smiling. He said in Hausa: "*Kai soja, iska lafiya*"—Hey soldier, wind is healthy. Or perhaps he meant, "May the wind give you health." I'm not sure. The gendarme simply waved back, and Issoufou, holding his smile, nodded and unhooked the rope from a wooden post. Just to be sure, perhaps to make the return trip a little easier, Issoufou walked over to the gendarme and stuffed a folded five-hundred-franc bill in a side pocket of the greatcoat.

The gendarme never looked up.

Road Journal

TANOUT, JANUARY 2, 1993. Issoufou's driving very hard today. Clocked him at 85 mph on road to Tanout. Christ! He's daring the road, playing roulette with damned cattle and goats crossing roads, and our lives. Animals wander across at any time and he never slows down. He's going to kill us! Can't write any more.

ZINDER, JANUARY 9. Niger radio reported a few days ago that Tuaregs attacked Tanout and two villages. That's on the old Zinder-Agadez road, 95 miles north of Zinder. They burned a Dutch project car in the town itself—in broad daylight, no less! Car was a Toyota Land Cruiser. This, Issoufou and other drivers tell me, is the first attack to penetrate the Zinder region.

JANUARY 11. Learned that Tuaregs burned three gas tankers on Route 2, 50 kilometers west of Agadez in December. The national radio says they stole a 504 station wagon and took the passengers 25 kilometers into the desert. They robbed and left them. Army patrol found the passengers hours later, apparently okay, though some men say they were beaten. The rebels took the driver with them, though it is unclear why.

Issoufou tells me the Tuaregs scare him. He will only drive during the day now so we are back in Zinder by 7:00 P.M. I'm not sure the road is any safer in daylight but I'm not telling Issoufou that.

JANUARY 18, 1993. A member of Niger's parliament showed up at the hostel today. He is Mohammed Musa Nguru, a self-described career "car trader" cum politician. Nguru says he travels to Maradi and Zinder 4–5 times a year to buy cars that he resells in Niamey and Ouagadougou (Burkina Faso). Says he bought two old Land Rovers and a Peugeot today and is now looking for drivers to take them to Niamey. I offered my services, but he laughed. "Too many problems. You don't have the right papers." I showed him my international driver's license (issued in Pennsylvania by AAA), and he shook his head, amused.

"No, no, I mean these papers." Nguru drew a wad of CFA, with a few U.S. one-dollar bills, from his pocket. A rubber band bound the bills. He held them up. We both laughed. I told him he was right. I did not have enough of the right papers.

MARADI AND ZINDER, FEBRUARY 1. On Maradi bush taxi run with Issoufou today. The checkpoints have maybe four or five more soldiers each, and all are armed with pistols or machine guns. Normally see only one weapon per checkpoint. The rebels are obviously having an impact, but we saw no patrols on the open road.

We took Issoufou's newest car, his third Peugeot station wagon. It is a 1971 model he bought from another driver in Maradi. Issoufou says he was the first driver in Zinder licensed to have a 504 bush taxi. In 1985 road accidents led the government to ban station wagons and sedans for use as bush taxis. They were too fast. When Kountché died, the government lifted the ban.

When we left this morning, Issoufou said, "I'm going to Mecca for sure now." But he still lacks insurance papers for the new car, and this cost him 500 CFA at every checkpoint into Maradi, about 6,500 francs total today. By nightfall, back in Zinder, Issoufou was angry, barely speaking. The checkpoint fees halved his 12,000 CFA fare profits. On our way back to Zinder, he feared the gendarmes would charge him a second time, but they didn't.

The extortion pattern is so inconsistent. I wonder if the gendarmes have a code that tells them how far they can push drivers and passengers. Or maybe today they just felt more powerful with their guns. At one checkpoint, I saw a gendarme with a CFA bill (could not tell what amount) sticking out from under his green beret. Never seen that before. Did he have a stash under the hat? Or was the bill a status symbol meant to be seen by fellow gendarmes?

We passed by each checkpoint and most gendarmes just waved us through for the return trip. Issoufou waved back, smiling and murmuring, "My respect, my respect, you bastards." We laughed.

FEBRUARY 6. I'm returning to Niamey tomorrow. Found a ride in an American AID (Agency for International Development) car. It's safer. Need to get some distance from the road, from bush taxis and the craziness. Feeling guilty, but just can't deal with it right now—Issoufou's driving especially. Been on the road with him 3–4 times a week. Too much. Can't sleep well, even with beer. I need to preserve my sanity and my life. I told Issoufou there are other things I need to investigate in Niamey, which is true. I want to meet Keletigui Mariko.

And we caused him to enter into our mercy,
for he was of the righteous.

— Koran, sura 21

Listening to Mariko

Lieutenant Colonel Jean François Klobb's last journal entries betray exhaustion and disgust, as if he could not come to terms with what he was seeing. He had been pushing fifty men east across the West African Sahel for six weeks, day and night. On July 11, 1899, in Koran-Kalgo, a village in southern Niger, he wrote, "Arrived in burned village full of corpses. Two little girls hung from a branch. The odor was infectious. . . . Well water is poisoned by bodies."

Lieutenant Octave Meynier, Klobb's adjutant, kept a slightly more specific and emotional record of Koran-Kalgo. "A single look to the bottom of these wells is enough for me. Vague forms, tangled over each other. . . ."[1]

The precise words seemed beyond both men.

They stood on the freshly plotted course of an African highway that was marked by the detritus of La Mission Afrique Centrale—the object of Klobb's hunt. Eight French officers and 450 African conscripts assigned, "in the name of science and civilization,"[2] to survey and claim the central Sudan to Lake Chad for France, which had already taken much of Africa west of the Niger River. The Central African Mission, led by thirty-two-year-old Captain Paul Voulet, marched from Bamako (now capital of Mali) in November 1898. In December, along the Niger River, the expedition, paranoid and short of supplies, began to crumble.

Niger's Route 1 is historically rooted in greed and madness. In the first seven months of 1899, Captain Voulet's expedition marched, murdered, pillaged, and nearly disintegrated on or within a few miles of what would soon be Route 1 (construction began in 1900). This road—roads all over Africa—remains haunted by men in uniform, and by blood. Redundant checkpoints, appalling automobile accidents. Route 1 is a living monument to colonial ambition.

Klobb, ordered to relieve Voulet, began his quest in May. The facts survive in Klobb's and Meynier's journals, published together under the title *A la recherche de Voulet* in Paris in 1931. Dozens of burned villages; piles of decapitated corpses, heads strewn about; thirteen women dangling from limbs in a stand of baobab trees. Voulet shot soldiers who wasted ammunition. Between villages, Klobb's force followed a trail of bodies. Stragglers reported that porters pressed into service from villages were bayoneted when they became useless. Thousands of dead.

If the journals reveal anything of value, it is the integrity of witness, a progressive numbness, as though both men were overwhelmed by something they were desperate to explain but could not. At one village, Klobb wrote, "Village burned by Voulet."[3]

At Birni-Nkonni, a very large village that Voulet completely destroyed, Klobb wrote sparingly: "Very large, magnificent village. . . . I find but a few men. The village chief, hiding out in the area, sends a few kind words, some couscous and meat and three sheep, but he does not come. The guide he sent has run off to save himself, leaving his horse. . . . Voulet entered the village, killed a thousand men and women, took the seven hundred best women, the horses, the camels."

What astounded the colonel, that strict Catholic and distinguished officer, more than the destruction was the depth of the brutality—at the hands of Frenchmen! It is difficult to imagine what Klobb witnessed along the six-hundred-mile path that began, for him, along the Niger River in what is now western Niger. That his task became an obsession is evident in the increasing coldness of his journal entries. The atrocities humiliated him, challenged both his identity and the honor of France, which is to say, the honor of Klobb, educated to be an engineer, to be logical and loyal. A man of forty-one, bespectacled, thin, with a long mustache that matched his physique, he lived by military tradition and law. "It pains me to think," he wrote on June 11, "that officers could command such horror."[4]

By July, his entries had become lists, stripped of adjectives.

Keletigui Mariko, standing beside his Land Rover, shook his head. He reached for his cane and a water bottle behind the car's front seat and took a sip. Then, pointing at his driver, who was filling the radiator with water, he said, "I warn him and warn him, but he drives too fast." I smiled weakly to empathize, but Mariko glared at me as if I too had betrayed him. He raised a finger. "One day he'll kill us."

I walked out on the asphalt to stretch my legs. Sand skidded south across Route 1 and tugged at my trouser cuffs, as if asking me to follow. The sound mimicked car tires on a wet street. All around me the ground looked fuzzy under thirty-mile-per-hour winds. Beneath the grainy haze that hugged the ground, Route 1 resembled the vertebrae of a prehistoric beast, revealed by slow scouring of wind and sand. Nature's bulldozing. We had stopped on the edge of a village where the landscape offered nothing to stop the sand except a few acacia trees and dried-out prosopis bushes. I could not make out the horizon for the dull khaki sand and the dust-filled sky, which mirrored the land. Even the village's mud houses seemed to dissolve into the sand. Brown stubble of millet and sorghum poked through the low haze here and there, evidence of the recent pitiful harvest. Much of the Zinder region had been declared a drought zone the previous summer, forcing local government to plead for food aid. This was a landscape of surrender.

I was back in the Zinder region, this time with Mariko, whose name I first heard when Issoufou Garba mentioned him the evening we met with the marabout, Malam Shafi. I had called on Mariko in Niamey, hoping he would help me with questions of history. He proved a cranky eccentric, but the supremacy of his knowledge of the Sahel's history and anthropology was unchallenged. Mariko invited me to travel with him back to Zinder, his hometown. He had a house there and spent a few days every month inspecting reforestation projects in the Zinder region. We left two days later, and when we arrived in Zinder city, I went to see Issoufou at the motor park. He reported that bush taxi business was dwindling. I told him about Mariko and said I'd be back in a few weeks. "Save a place for me in your Peugeot," I said.

Issoufou seemed sad but smiled anyway. "No problem," he said.

Today, I had been traveling with Mariko since dawn, east from Zinder to visit a forestry project near the village of Gouré. He was angry. The anger sizzled softly, perpetually. All morning we had endured army checkpoints every few miles. At 9:00 A.M., when we stopped at the village to put water in the Land Rover's ailing radiator, Mariko expressed his frustration with the lethargic soldiers: "*Ils mangent ce pays.*"—They eat this country. And now with his driver, who, like most drivers in Africa, worshipped speed.

While Mariko was angry, I was shaken.

Twenty minutes before, motoring along at eighty miles an hour, we observed this: small figures far ahead, frantically flinging sand on the road. Closing in, we saw six children, including a girl in a green head cloth and wrap, scooping sand into potholes with their hands. They leaped in the road, laughing, waving, jumping about. The driver never slowed. He smiled, lowered the window, and drew from his breast pocket a handful of yellow coins—five-, ten-, twenty-five-franc pieces—that he flung out the window as we passed, forcing a boy to leap out of our way. Over my shoulder, I watched the coins bounce and glitter in the hazy sun. The children dove for them, kicking, swinging at one another, getting up and diving again.

A tiny profit from the road. The driver chuckled. I winced. Mariko bowed his head.

Mariko is a link between the road and its past.

You begin with his name, Keletigui, a Bambara word (the language of Mali) that means "master of war." It is the name of his father, who came to Niger from Mali. Mariko was seventy-four when I met him, born in Zinder, a city his father first entered wearing the uniform of an African *tirailleur*—a foot soldier in blue tunic and baggy red pantaloons. Sergeant Keletigui accompanied Klobb on the hunt for Voulet. Afterward, he married and retired a pensioner, a man due the respect owed to one who landed on the right side of colonial conflicts.

His son, Mariko, studied in colonial schools, trained as a veterinarian in Dakar, Senegal, French West Africa's administrative capital, and entered the colonial veterinary service in 1946. He worked across the French Sudan—Mali, Upper Volta (now Burkina Faso), Niger, and later for his country's government. He learned six languages walking the bush with farmers, herdsmen, and hunters, training to be a warrior in an environmental struggle.

You find the link in his writing, like this poem fragment (translated from the French):

> Like the nomad, I dream of an Africa without frontiers,
> Of a united Africa liberated from police harassment
> And formalities imported from another continent.[5]

He has published poems, a novel, three natural history books, dozens of articles, and a memoir that is still read in Niger's secondary schools. While treating cattle diseases, advising farmers on goat feed, trapping poisonous snakes—a means to support his passionate curiosity—Mariko studied rural life, spiritual hunting rituals, the stratigraphy and chemistry of the land. He explored what he calls in his memoir, *Souvenirs de la boucle du Niger,* "a martyr region,"[6] the Sahel, a place of environmental decay. Centuries of overgrazing and cutting trees for cropland—encouraged by tradition and policy—exacerbated a drought that has never fully lifted.

In 1981, Mariko co-founded the aid agency SOS Sahel International, under whose auspices he travels by foot and Land Rover, talking about gardens and trees. Spend enough time on the roads, he says, and you can sense how things are by the number of checkpoints and the soldiers' moods; by the state of the landscape and how much of the road disappears under shifting sands.

On his feet, Mariko seems to glide, legs concealed beneath a long cotton robe, gray for the field and white for the office, as he plants his cane deliberately step for step. A strong and trim man with thin gray hair. The cane is like classroom chalk, used to point and to make diagrams in the sand. He is "West Africa's senior veterinarian" (his words). He'll also tell you: "*Je suis géologue, paléontologue, anthropologue.*" He won't talk politics, though contempt for government surfaces through his carefully enunciated French. "Ministers call grand meetings on reforestation, but do nothing!" The last word pops. It hangs in the air like a puff of smoke.

His policy critiques appear in newspapers and journals in Africa and France. In 1978, General Kountché threw him in jail. After Mariko had spent a few days in a crowded cell, the general summoned him. "Kountché called me in to discuss agriculture. I told him my views are known. I sign everything I write and stand by it. He freed me after five days." Mariko never found out why he'd been arrested. But the government continued harassing him, challenging his citizenship, summoning him to explain articles, occasionally detaining him, until Kountché died. In the 1980s, Mariko accused Mali of abusing the human rights of Tuareg nomads. His articles were banned there until the government fell in 1991 and the ruling general, Moussa Traore, was imprisoned.

I decided, while waiting for Mariko and the driver, to walk a bit on this road that seems so timid, fraying badly at the edges and rutted in places, like a country road in southern Idaho. An hour may go by before a car passes. Route 1 is a relic of colonial lust, a road like many the Europeans built in Africa, designed to lead *out* more than lead *in*. My government map of Niger showed that Route 1's center collapses in a giant V to the south—to the coast—near the border with Benin (600 miles west of where I stood), where another road goes to the railhead 190 miles across the frontier at Parakou. The rail line, built in the 1920s, connects the interior to the seaport of Cotonou. Once, the railroad was part of a giant suction system for cotton, palm oil, grain, labor, military conscripts. The French feared the project wouldn't pay and never finished it. The train still runs between Cotonou and Parakou under a name that preserves hope: Organisation Commune Benin-Niger. Likewise, Route 1 is an odd presence on the land. Perhaps it is the road's persistent narrowness and silence, its character of seeming to be something the French failed to pack up and take with them when they left.

History tends to ambush here. In 1986, in a village market one morning, a woman grabbed her young son by the shoulders and pointed at me. "*Tu vois, tu vois*," she said—You see, you see—"*c'est le capitaine Voulet.*" She laughed as the boy struggled. He looked at me wide-eyed, kicking and screaming. When I told a Nigerien friend about it, he smiled. "When I was bad," he explained, "my mother told me Captain Voulet would come and eat me. She never said who Voulet was, just that he would eat me."

Schoolteachers in Niger talk about "*l'histoire de Voulet-Chanoine,*" after the commander and his adjutant, Captain Charles Chanoine. I learned the story from a student when I was a Peace Corps teacher in Bouza, where the woman called me "*le capitaine Voulet.*" Just the appearance of a car in Bouza was a notable event. I imagined the spectacle of a European military column passing a few miles south eighty-seven years earlier, close to where Route 1 is now.

By 1899, a patchwork of European powers controlled much of Africa's coast. The French were moving across the continent, riding a wave of humiliation born of defeat in the Franco-Prussian War of 1870. National honor had to be restored. The British, moreover, had ceded the Sahara to France and laughed about it, boasting of having surrendered only sand. France, as if to prove its virility, annexed parts of North, West, and Central Africa.

In the summer of 1899, three French expeditions were closing on Lake Chad from the south, the north, and the west—Voulet's Central African Mission—to secure Central Africa and the mineral wealth they hoped to find. It was a time of transition. Ten years had passed since the United States Army had crushed the last serious Native American resistance. The Greco-Turkish and Spanish-American wars had recently ended. European and American engineers were competing to develop automobile technology. And Armand Peugeot was just refining designs for the line of cars to be manufactured by a newly incorporated company, the Société Anonyme des Automobiles Peugeot.

The Central African Mission story stayed with me, preserved in my maps of Niger. Route 1 dominates the transport geography; it is a determined red line that looks more like a battered spine than an artery. The road crosses a vast, flat terrain stripped by people and nature—the hand of agriculture, the rub of wind and water.

Palm, acacia, and baobab forests have disintegrated here. Good soil, vulnerable without grassy cover, surrenders to wind. Some baobabs stand with roots exposed, the innards of an eroding ecology, grotesque and apocalyptic, elevated a few feet above the earth that once buried them. The most visually remarkable wildlife— giraffes and elephants, for instance—is largely gone from this plain marked by blobs of volcanic rock and laterite scabs. Underskin laid open, raw and hot, like second-degree burns.

Voulet and Klobb encountered a much greener savanna peppered by trees and animal herds. Hyenas followed Voulet's column, preying on stragglers and feeding on the dead the column left in its wake. Yet it was still a land of extreme heat and wind, punctuated by summer monsoons, three or four months of patchy rains that both nurtured crops and washed them away with swift violence. Wind and dust off the Sahara to the north often cloaked the land and the French officers in white grit.

A door slammed behind me. I walked back to the Land Rover. Mariko was waiting beside the car, his wooden cane hooked over his wrist. He threw glances at me and then delivered an awkward declaration, a sort of non sequitur apology for his angry complaints about his driver: "If there are people who say I'm indefatigable, it's because they know that despite my age, even when I'm one hundred and fifteen, I'll still be out here doing this." He pounded his sandaled feet to emphasize walking, contact with the land. Then he got in the car. The driver and I followed suit.

On the road, Mariko often meets with extension agents. They accompany him on foot to project sites hundreds of yards, sometimes a mile or two, into the bush. The agents, men in their twenties and thirties, struggle to keep pace with him. They call Mariko *le docteur*, a formal academic title and, in Mariko's case, an affectionate nickname. As Mariko walks, he lectures on science and history. He begins with *"Mon père m'a dit que..."* (for example, "My father told me this area was lush and green and the people strong and healthy"), or "I first came here in 1940." Sometimes he talks of Klobb, *"un officier intègre"*—an officer of integrity—"who tried to stop the madness." Mariko owns a copy of the Klobb-Meynier journals. "I visited every old bookseller in Paris to find a copy," he told me.

Pieces of the Central African Mission's story decay in government archives in Niamey and elsewhere around Niger. In Zinder, a tiny building behind the provincial governor's office houses tens of thousands of pages: colonial reports on politics, religion, botany, geology, agriculture, and military matters dating from 1899 until independence in 1960. A broad three-foot-high mound on the floor. The material gathers dust, termites, and scorpions, yellow scorpions that scurry out when you pick up a book or piece of paper.

That day, driving east from Zinder, Mariko the eyewitness worked his memory for me. "I don't like questions in the car," he said. "Just let me talk." After a while, he said: "When I was four [in 1923], my parents began sending me to visit relatives in Kournawa [sixty miles west of Zinder on the road]. French officers would come to the village with soldiers to collect people for labor battalions. They would walk through the village with the chief—I remember this—calling people from their homes. Men, women, older children, boys, girls, it didn't matter. Most worked the road. They carried laterite. They ground it up to repair rough sections or parts the rains had washed out. Many died. Many didn't get enough food or water. They beat them, too. But my father had been a soldier, so I never had to go." He stopped there.

I read the Klobb-Meynier journals, too, Mariko's copy, spending afternoons with my notebooks, maps, and the journals spread on a table in his office. The room is stuffed with bookshelves, wall maps of West Africa and Niger. He owns rare editions of early European scientific studies of Africa, including the reports of the Tilho mission, a French team of geologists, anthropologists, and botanists who crossed Niger by camel in 1906, traveling along the Niger River just as Route 1 does, and then east. Every flat surface in his office supports fossils, books, paper, scattered jars containing insect specimens, and snakes preserved in formaldehyde—vipers and cobras Mariko trapped himself. It bothered me, I finally told him, how closely the national highway follows Captain Voulet's route, west to east. He smiled. "Yes, you'll find the road connects many things in our past."

The only pictures I know of Lieutenant Colonel Klobb and Captain Voulet are two drawings printed in textbooks used in Niger's secondary schools and in the book *Le grand capitaine*, by the French journalist Jacques-Francis Rolland.[7] Klobb, a military martinet in a pince-nez and long, waxed gray mustache, stands in a marine artillery officer's dress uniform before a lace-covered table, gloved left hand atop his sword. Voulet, chin raised under a close-cut black mustache, wears four decorations across his chest. There is tradition and order in the first drawing, blunt ambition in the face in the second.

From December to March, before Klobb's hunt began, Voulet's courier dispatches to the governor-general complained vaguely of inadequate water and supplies, the treachery of villagers, of imminent attack from Tuareg nomads whom he believed had infiltrated the villages. The dispatches did not detail the solutions pursued in the field, but it seems possible Voulet was preparing a defense of his actions—planting the idea that, to feed his men, he had no choice but to forcibly take what he needed.

The violence disgusted several of Voulet's officers, though they were afraid to question him. A lieutenant dismissed early in the mission for lack of discipline described atrocities in letters home to France. They were given to a government minister. And the commander of the Niger River post at Say, Captain Granderye, challenged Voulet's actions. Granderye surveyed the destruction along the river, talked to villagers. He found that the villages had welcomed the expedition, only to be sacked. "The left bank of the Niger River to [the village of] Sansané Haoussa has been put to fire and blood," he wrote the governor-general in March. Claims of a Tuareg threat, he added, "are completely false. There are no Tuaregs here. . . . Our influence, the prestige of France are gone in this region."[8]

In February, Voulet turned east, away from the river, along a path parallel to the border with British Nigeria. He chose the southern route to avoid Tuareg territory closer to the desert, and because he hoped to find more water.

To the casual witness, maybe a farmer looking up from his field, the expedition must have seemed a fantastic visual anomaly. Powerful, wonderfully foreign, terrifying, like a great parade gone drunkenly awry. First, on horseback, rode a line of eight white men in white uniforms, tight tunics and trousers. Black-visored kepis with gold or red stripes of rank shielded their heads. They wore leather riding gloves and high leather boots. From the waist of each man hung a sword in its scabbard and a holstered pistol, though the farmer would not have recognized many of these things. Then he would have seen a column of Africans in blue tunics and red pantaloons, marching with rifles shouldered. Finally, he would have been bewildered or frightened when he saw the supply train: a procession, stretching a mile or more, of emaciated camels, donkeys, porters and their families, women taken for the soldiers' pleasure, plodding on foot or astride beasts, the weak clinging to the backs of the strong. These, the farmer's own people, some two thousand souls altogether.[9]

Many villagers would have had time only to see soldiers—drafted from villages across the colonies—running them down with bayonets fixed. This while the officers, a distant white line on horseback, watched.

Advance surveyors of a road.

Mariko sat up straight in the Land Rover, looking ahead, ignoring the young soldier who wanted to see his identity card. The man was snapping his fingers inches from Mariko's ear, something a young Nigerien would seldom do with an elder were he not given the artificial authority of a uniform and sidearm. "*Carte, carte*," the soldier said. Mariko softly asked, "Where is your sense of dignity?" The soldier folded his arms. "I'm a citizen," Mariko said, "more of a citizen than you'll ever be." The driver sighed, as if to say, "Okay, here we go." The soldier opened the door. He said, "Get out."

I had seen this sort of thing before. A passenger's stubbornness, demands for rights, then brief violence—a fist, a boot, a soldier's drawn gun. The nature of African road checkpoints.

We were at the checkpoint in Gouré, forty miles east of our water stop. Mariko might have surrendered his documents in another country, but this was Niger. The soldier waited, arms loose at his sides and hesitant to step forward to touch Mariko, sensing, possibly, a situation he might not be able to control. He was not used to such challenges, and perhaps he saw something in Mariko's age and demeanor, in the fact that Mariko had resumed reading a book open on his lap, *Le théâtre de Sophocles*. The soldier began to shuffle uncomfortably, like a student awaiting a grade.

Mariko looked at the soldier and pointed behind him, to a peasant woman crossing a field astride a donkey. In an even voice he lectured. "There," he said, "there is a citizen who has a real identity and real rights." The soldier turned to look. Mariko asked in Hausa, "*Kai bahaushe ne?*"—You're Hausa, aren't you? The man nodded. He was young, fresh; he smiled nervously. Mariko aimed his words at the soldier's roots, probably a farm village. He continued in Hausa: "That woman works with her hands. She bears many children. She starves during drought, but has never stolen a thing." The soldier stared back. "And you," Mariko added, "what do you do? What achievements can you claim? You haven't the integrity to occupy the same space as that woman." A pause, and then, in French, he said, "*Tire sur moi si tu veux . . .*"—Shoot me if you like, but I will not hand you my papers. They watched each other, Mariko the professor awaiting a response, and the soldier unsure how to reply.

Finally, the young man frowned and waved us on. "Go on," he said, and walked over to unhook the rope strung between two posts across the road.

Mariko turned to me in the backseat. "Often they take a woman off a bush taxi because of some 'problem' with her papers. They tell the taxi to go, and then rape her." He spoke slowly; he wanted this to sink in. "I've seen women's bodies in ditches along the road after they used them. The families never dare protest."

We continued to Gouré in silence. I did not utter a comment or ask a question for fear of cheapening Mariko's small victory. It occurred to me, looking at Mariko sitting straight and correct in the Land Rover, that he carried on a struggle that Klobb had begun nearly a century earlier.

"I'm worried," Mariko said. The Land Rover bounced over hard track three miles north of Gouré and Route 1. The village wells here gave plenty of water, and Mariko envisioned garden and forestry projects, which, if successful, would serve as models for the region. "We are looking at the very last trees. Soon there will be nothing here but sand." The only plant relief was an occasional baobab or palm tree and patches of prosopis bushes in rocky ravines.

The vehicle was full now, carrying a forester and extension official from the district government offices in Gouré, men in their mid-twenties wearing European shirts and trousers. They nodded gravely at Mariko, but struggled with me to imagine what the old man remembered. They had come to absorb his ideas and offer what they knew. "I first visited this area in 1946," Mariko said. "It was all green."

The Land Rover slowed near the base of a sandy ridge, half a mile across, where Mariko called a halt before we reached loose sand. On foot, we followed him a couple of hundred feet to the very foot of the ridge, not far from a large baobab. The wind molded his robe to his legs in front and flapped it behind him. He pointed his cane at the ridge-top. "The French camped there after they left Zinder. Lieutenant Meynier's journal describes a verdant land that was grassy and forested to the horizon." The two officials had heard this before. They shifted and sighed, uncomfortable in the sun. Mariko talked with his back to us, and I suspected he knew how impatient the men were. On the ride out, in front of them, he told me, "When I'm talking to officials responsible for projects, I try to determine whether they reflect—even for a moment—on the meaning of rural development, on history and what this land once was and what it should be, and on the needs of the people."

The men nodded respectfully, but now, standing in the sand, one whispered to me. "When you are well fed and healthy your whole life it's easy to have energy, but we who live at the bottom—" He shrugged.

Mariko's words interested me, but I sympathized with the officials. We walked a land that blinds the eyes and mind, a land whose harshness I respected but would never grow accustomed to. This environment sucks up energy and patience. No African in this group but Mariko knew a broad, productive landscape like the one Meynier had observed and Klobb had ridden across not far to the west. I lusted for contrast, for something green or purple, anything, a palm grove or lawn, and I was startled at how pleasing I found the fantasy of a golf course, whose controlled, artificial nature repels me in my own country.

We had fallen behind Mariko, who was waiting beside the baobab. The tree stood perhaps forty feet high, with a great gray trunk and bare limbs that grew wide and high. Its roots rose four feet above the sand, exposing the wide, twisted dome the roots formed as they reached briefly outward and then thrust deep. The Hausa attribute special powers to great trees, which may explain why this tree survived cutting, only to suffer the indignity of the wind revealing the secret of its root system. "I know this tree." Mariko was looking at the forester and extension agent now. "I knew it as a child." I sensed what was coming, a lecture that played on fear, guilt. "Six years ago these roots were beneath soil." He knocked them with his cane. "This land was forested, but villagers cut trees for farms and firewood. Young people like you, I fear for you. How are you going to eat? I fear there is no future."

No one responded.

After a while, Mariko started back to the Land Rover and we followed him. "Hassan," he said to the forester, "tell me how the villagers are doing with their tree nurseries."

The end was pathetic.

Klobb's scouts tracked Voulet and ran him to earth near Tessaoua. The colonel sent four soldiers to tell the captain he was relieved of his command. Voulet sent the soldiers back to Klobb with a written reply: "I will treat you as an enemy if you continue your march against me. I am resolved to sacrifice my life."[10] It was July 11. Earlier that same day, Klobb had ridden through Koran-Kalgo and seen its wells filled with the dead.

After receiving Voulet's message, Klobb decided to close in on the captain. And Voulet, for his part, took a detachment from the mission's main camp and rode out to find and confront the colonel. The two forces sighted one another outside the village of Dankori on Bastille Day, July 14.

The officers met on opposite sides of a field. Klobb, his detachment flying the French tricolor, appealed again. Voulet ordered his men to fire on Klobb, who had told his men to hold their fire. Captain Voulet was, after all, a French officer, and one French officer, Klobb had hoped, would not shoot another. Voulet reportedly pointed a pistol at his soldiers as he gave the order to fire. Klobb, a bullet in his head, died with several of his men. Voulet fled. Two days later, Voulet's soldiers—angered by his threat to shoot deserters—shot him and Captain Chanoine at the village of May Jirgui, a spot today split by the road.

The two captains are entombed there in decaying concrete enclosed in an iron fence behind the village, just south of the road. No one maintains the graves; the village chief keeps the iron name markers.

Lieutenant Meynier, slightly wounded in the leg, joined the surviving officers of the Central African Mission. They had gained control of the expedition and were continuing east. Klobb was eventually buried with honors in Timbuktu, where he had been commandant. A small cement memorial to him stands at the Tessaoua prefecture on Route 1. Beneath his name is the inscription "Died for France."

The findings of the military inquest—a copy is in the National Archives of Niger with the investigation reports—echo with panic, with frantic rationalization that invites, first, a reader's impatience, and later, incredulity. The record regards Paul Voulet as an officer of "courage and intelligence," led astray by ambition. The inquest absolved the surviving officers of responsibility.[11]

You read, shake your head.

The record concedes that Voulet declared himself—in a speech to his men after killing Klobb—"a black chief," founder of a bush empire that would rival France and drain the mother country's military and economic resources.

You squirm a little.

Sympathizers to the colonial cause push Voulet's defense with impressive imagination, blaming an illness called—depending on the preferred term—*la soudanite* or *le cafard*,[12] a peculiar, vague form of nervous psychosis brought on by Africa—the relentless heat and wind, disease, the difficulty of getting on in a harsh climate. The words surface in the testimony of the investigating officers. The anonymous preface to the Klobb-Meynier journals explains: "It is this state of absolute agitation with so many small causes that produces such regrettable effects."

At this, you might laugh.

Road Journal

MARCH 5, 1993. Arrived in Zinder with Mariko last night. Found Issoufou Garba at motor park this morning, sipping coffee. One of his cars is down with engine trouble and he has no money for repairs. He also says that many days he and his other driver cannot get enough passengers to make a run anywhere. Issoufou blames the government. He may have a point. Civil servants, soldiers are not getting paid at all. Less cash circulating.

He told me: "It is good you found me when you did. Bush taxis are not working now."

MARCH 8. Early morning visit to Mirria market with Mariko, 12 miles east of Zinder on Route 1. He's at home in Mirria market, his "favorite childhood place." He walked the market like the proprietor, right hand moving his cane, left hand behind his back.

We walked through crowds where tailors and leather workers call him to inspect their material. "Mariko, Mariko!" It was as if a visit from him proved the quality of a merchant's products. In adjacent field, a livestock yard, he walked among horses, camels, donkeys all of which have hind feet hobbled by rope. Mariko bent to inspect hooves, or soothe an animal, his hands on its face to allow him to see its teeth. He made simple examinations, asking brief questions. "How often do you feed him?" Or, to the owner of a camel resting in sand, "Her eye is badly infected." He moved from animal to animal with an entourage, the animal owners, following like hospital interns.

Mariko said that when he was a child, teachers at the Zinder primary school chose the best students to visit Mirria market every week. He was one of them, of course. The Mirria market straddles Route 1 and is one of Niger's oldest and largest. Merchants told me the market is pushing 150 years in age.

"Teachers asked us to identify market goods and describe them," Mariko told me. "We had to try to find out where goods came from, and to find those places on the map. The market was a giant classroom in geography and history and economics. We found metal pots from eastern Europe, matches from France, tea from Algeria, cotton and pineapple and sugar from Nigeria and Cameroon, and vegetables from around Niger. Many of these were places that I had never heard of."

We passed a woman selling vegetables spread on ground cloth; beside her sat a man with music cassettes stacked on cloth, dozens of them in neat rows. Mariko picked up a Rod Stewart tape (probably a pirate version from Nigeria). He smiled at me. "The market has changed a little."

> Men are superior to women on account of the qualities
> with which God hath gifted one above the other.
>   — Koran, sura 4

A Woman at the Wheel

I should have been talking with Hajia Mariatou Moustapha. We had an appointment. Instead, I was watching her shoulder through a throng of angry men standing around a body on the ground outside the central market in Niamey. She was shouting, "*Laissez lui, laissez lui.*"—Leave him alone, leave him alone.

But four men, shorter and thinner than she—it took at least four—gripped her arms and shoulders and hustled Mariatou backward out of the crowd. She shuffled back with them, not struggling and somehow not surprised, but shaking her head and saying something I couldn't hear. The men left her standing alone on the street and returned to the crowd. She watched the mob carry the body of the man she sought, hoisted shoulder high on many hands, to an unknown fate.

It mattered to no one except Mariatou that the so-called thief never had a chance to plead his case, that he may, in fact, have been innocent. He had been caught in situ, on the edge of the open marketplace, opening the driver's-side door of her car, a Peugeot 504 station wagon, brand new. Not hers, really, but her employer's, the United Nations Children's Fund. Hajia Mariatou is Niger's only licensed woman commercial driver, and possibly the only one in West Africa. And everyone, as she would be the first to tell you, knows her around this city.

Someone saw this "thief" and, having recognized the car he was opening, the witness shouted, "*Voleur, voleur!*"—Thief, thief!—a death sentence in a West African market where the crowds, the chatter, the odors and sounds of business and society run thick. Someone sent a boy to fetch Mariatou from inside the market, where she operates a driving school from a one-room office. Mariatou teaches people how to drive, another first for a Nigerien woman. Her clients are mostly other women (she hired a man to handle the male clients), though she teaches the occasional man, usually one wealthy enough not to care who knows a woman is telling him how to drive.

A taxi had dropped me off outside the market's high cement walls in time to catch sight of this woman wading into the mob around the accused, her head, loosely bound in fashionable blue cloth, bobbing above the crowd. As I approached, I saw the four men carry her back. From the edge of the crowd, I saw the alleged thief lying under clubs, fists, feet. Ashen faced. Blood pooled in the pit of the man's neck above his collarbone and poured from his nose and forehead. Pink foam caked his lips. His arm was broken, bent crazily backward at the elbow.

For a couple of minutes Mariatou observed this scene, the palm of her right hand over her mouth, before she turned, head bowed, and walked away. She carried a certain authority that allowed her to face down a crowd of men, and a certain common sense that told her not to struggle when the men carried her out. Mariatou was thirty-seven years old, five feet ten inches tall, and around two hundred pounds, a size she cultivated. She walked gracefully and swiftly, elbows out, in her bright blue cotton wrap and matching robe. On her right forearm, six gold and silver bracelets clinked faintly when she swung her arms. I followed her back to the office, l'École Conduite Mariatou, where I had hoped to interview her. The room, located in a corner of the market's cement walls, was windowless and furnished with a wooden table, two chairs, and a six-foot-high diagram of city streets and traffic symbols painted in blue, yellow, white, and red on one wall. Mariatou sat, her face drawn, but she smiled weakly. She said, "I think you should come back in the morning."

"Men can't do everything," Hajia Mariatou told me when I first met her in early April 1993, three weeks before the market incident. We were in the Peugeot, driving across Niamey on UNICEF errands, the first of many rides I took with her around the city. "Teaching people to drive made me restless, so my husband said, 'Why don't you drive a city bus and teach them what a woman can do?'" This grant of independence struck me as out of the ordinary in a Muslim marriage, but Mariatou saw the situation simply. She gave me a look of surprised annoyance when I inquired about it. "He is a generous and good man," she said.

At the wheel, Mariatou is aggressive, deft with the stick shift and heavy on horn and gas pedal. I had come to accept this sort of driving in Africa, where road laws are few. I was impressed by the contrast between Mariatou's speed, the sharpness of her turns, and the steady calm on her face. This is how one survives on the roads of an African city, where each roadway is its own marketplace stuffed with buyers and traders whose mobile business dealings spill right into traffic. Vendors port stacks of cloth, trays of meat or tea, cut limes. Children, goats, and dogs dart out from nowhere. Mariatou smiled at me. "So many village people come here to the city and they don't understand the risks of the street. They don't know about cars." She did not slow down as she said this, and we never had an accident.

I had been in Niger eight months at that point, hanging out with an all-male cast of drivers, gendarmes, and *komasho*. And my main informant, of course, was a man, Issoufou Garba. African road transport exists by men and for men. Women tag along, going to market to buy and sell, to visit relatives, to take children to the hospital—where, in this poor and drought-stricken country, they often die. Malnutrition, malaria, meningitis. . . .

I wanted to know what travel was like for an African woman, to see the situation from her point of view if possible. For a Western man, though, getting such knowledge was not easy. I found it difficult, for instance, to talk with individual women without attracting unwanted attention or having my intentions misinterpreted. "Do you want my daughter?" a man would ask. Or, "Monsieur, are you looking for a wife?" Women would not talk to me alone anyway. So I spoke to women in groups or in the presence of their husbands, sons, and brothers, until I met Hajia Mariatou.

In Zinder, I had asked Issoufou about women bush taxi drivers. "There aren't any," he said. "There is a woman in Niamey who drives a city bus. I saw her on television." On the subject of women drivers, he was noncommittal. "If women want to drive bush taxis, let them," he said. A safe opinion. Issoufou knew women wouldn't pose a competitive threat anytime soon. In any case, he did not think it was a subject worth exploring.

In Niamey, a national bus company official told me the woman I sought had taken a job at UNICEF. I called on Mariatou at UNICEF headquarters one morning without an appointment. I explained how I had learned of her, my interest in her story, and told her I wanted to write about her. She received me warmly and invited me to go along on her morning rounds in her UNICEF Peugeot. I noticed, clipped to the car's sun visor, a photo portrait of her in her old job at the wheel of a city bus. At her driving school office, a framed copy of the photo hangs on a wall in a superior position—above the ubiquitous picture of the head of Niger's army (which looks out from every office, shop, hotel, and restaurant in the country, a reminder to the population of who would rule if the civilian government let things get out of hand).

As we rolled away from the UNICEF compound, Mariatou began to tell me about her wish to start her own bush taxi service. "Bush taxis don't take care of what women need," she said. "I know a woman who was thrown off a bush taxi in the middle of the night with her two children because she insisted the driver take her home, just a kilometer from the main road. The driver got out and pulled them out of the taxi. He threw their baggage out on the road. She screamed at the driver, but he laughed at her." Mariatou told this story without emotion. It was, after all, a common example of an African woman's life, a sample injustice, but one that stuck with her. Her acquaintance walked home safely that night. Mariatou wanted me to understand that women drivers would be welcome at her taxi line; she could train them herself. And the needs of women passengers would be honored. Her taxis would allow ample space for women and their children; nor would her drivers leave women stranded on city streets at night. And since many women travel to bring their children to medical treatment, Mariatou would offer more transport to dispensaries and clinics.

It's not that all male drivers are a threat, Mariatou said. Some do accommodate women's demands, driving the extra distance to home or market or clinic. I had seen a few do that, too. "But it usually does not work this way," she added. She raised her finger for emphasis. "Money, that is the big problem," she said. "I can't do this alone, and no one has money to give, not even my husband. No one has money these days."

We stopped at the government-owned beverage distributor to buy four cases of Coca-Cola for a UNICEF reception. She impatiently gave orders to the two men loading the cases in the car's rear ("No, put them beside each other, not on top"). We went to the Ministry of Health to pick up documents; and then to the Banque Internationale de l'Afrique Occidental, where the bank director had an envelope for her; and finally we stopped at a parts shop where she paid for a dozen new spark plugs and fuel filters for the UNICEF motor pool.

On our way to the shop on the city's broad Boulevard Charles de Gaulle, a man driving a Mercedes sedan cut us off, forcing Mariatou to hit her brakes hard to avoid a collision. She raised her right hand and, as if flicking water or something much more unpleasant, threw all five fingers at him in a gesture of grave insult, hoping he would see her in his rearview mirror as he drove away. But the car just faded into the distance. Mariatou said nothing.

I can't be sure that Hajia Mariatou (she took the title "Hajia" after making the Muslim pilgrimage to Mecca in 1985) is, in fact, West Africa's only licensed woman commercial driver. It seems likely that a few women drive city taxis, buses, or bush taxis elsewhere in West Africa. But when I checked, during my travels, with transport authorities in Nigeria, Mali, Ivory Coast, Burkina Faso, Sierra Leone, Benin, and Togo, my search turned up not one. Once, in northern Nigeria, on a street in Kaduna, I saw a woman driving a Toyota minibus stuffed with people and baggage, a typical bush taxi. The bus stopped on a street for a passenger. I sprinted after the vehicle as it sped away, but in vain.

In Africa, women commonly drive their own cars, but not commercial vehicles. I found a few women who owned bush taxis, city taxis, and trucks, but these women didn't drive. They did business shrewdly, defensively, in perpetual conflict with the men they hire to drive and with the soldiers at checkpoints. Hajia Mariatou wants to do both—be a driver and own a transport company.

During the 1970s, Mariatou taught primary school, but she got bored. She wanted to drive and asked her husband to teach her. He helped her get a job at the Niamey city bus line. "He told me I could drive better than any of the men they had." She remained there for four years. As a UNICEF driver, a job she found without help, she is mostly an errand runner—a prime job, a rare and lucrative find in the dusty capital of a country plagued by economic stagnation, drought, and food shortages. A fine-tuned, comfortable, air-conditioned car with a stereo radio-cassette player is a choice work environment in one of the world's hottest capital cities.

Mariatou is mother to two boys and three girls, and is the second of El Haji Moustapha Garba's four wives. El Haji Garba, a construction materials dealer and son of a Hausa merchant family, travels Africa and Europe on business. He speaks excellent French, circulates in Niamey's community of diplomats and development workers, and is a devout Muslim. He allows his wives a measure of freedom, a situation that benefits him, and perhaps his wives as well. The marriage arrangement works like a small corporation with a president (him) and four vice presidents. In 1980, El Haji Garba sent his first wife three hundred miles east to run the Hotel Guidan Moustapha, a tourist haven he built in Madaoua on Route 1. Mariatou, for her part, runs the driving school, which her husband started in the 1970s. Wives three and four handle the household, including twenty-some children and sales of milk and meat from a herd of thirty goats.

My interest in her story flattered Mariatou, but the attention also made her nervous. When I asked about her family, she said, "It's not necessary to talk about that." Mariatou does not figure in transport studies; she is an anomaly. Stacks of UN, World Bank, and African government studies on transport speak of "private capital inflows" in convoluted sentences: "Government intervention in the provision of public transport services has invariably been unsuccessful." A 1991 World Bank technical paper entitled "Intermediate Means of Transport in Sub-Saharan Africa" contains this passage about women: "Women almost exclusively transport water and biomass fuel in addition to the movement of harvested crops. . . . The role played by women in African transport industry varies from country to country. . . . They collect produce . . . arrange for its transport . . . and finally sell it."[1]

In fact, as several World Bank and other development agency reports note, African women do most of their traveling on foot. Women and children "head-load" much of the food transported across cities and through rural areas. African women carry between 70 and 90 percent of agricultural crops from the field to home or market. They carry almost all of the water for their families, and collect most of the wood fuel. But the reports mention nothing about women drivers or transport owners.

Niger's citizens, during the time of my visit, were for the first time since independence testing the limits of their freedom. Elections were scheduled and political parties were forming by the dozen; people beat thieves to death in the streets; bush taxi drivers and travelers openly challenged soldiers at checkpoints, refusing to pay bribes or even to show identity cards. Soldiers, overwhelmed by the new attitude, occasionally beat people, but most often they let them go. The army dismantled half the checkpoints on Route 1—for three months.

In Zinder, Muslim clerics called on men to stone women who did not wear head cloths and women whose cloth wraps hovered above their ankles. General Kountché and his governors, who had reserved gestures of authority for themselves, would have thrown the clerics in prison. Not now. I saw terrified girls and women running, stumbling under stones and fists, through the streets, through the motor parks, steps ahead of gangs of laughing men and boys.

One night, a mob of men and boys gathered with clubs and torches outside the new government women's center—a maverick institution where women gathered to talk and learn market and accounting skills, new crafts, even to type. After the women inside had fled, the men sacked the building, smashing its one computer. They carried off the half dozen manual typewriters and set the place afire. The head of the Zinder section of the Association des Femmes Nigeriènne told me the gendarmes ignored her pleas for help, even as the flames dominated the night sky.

Issoufou lives near the building. He showed me the burnt cement shell one morning, remarking at the shit that covered the floors, the charcoal phallic drawings on the walls. "This is all so crazy," he said. He was silent for the rest of the fifteen minutes we spent there, speaking only when we were walking away. "The honest men of the city were not involved in this. It was hoodlums," he said. "This kind of thing has never happened before in Niger." About the latter, at least, he was right.

Nigeriens in the early 1990s were enduring much that was new. The transitional civilian government, when it had money, paid soldiers and police first, but even they were months behind in receiving their pay, and the soldiers had the strongest means to extort it. People without identity cards made good targets at checkpoints, particularly women, who almost never carried the cards.

In this poor rural country, where government has few resources, many laws go unnoticed or ignored. To get identity cards, women usually apply through husbands or male relatives, who bear witness to their identity. This means a woman must ask her husband, brother, or father to help her get a card. The men question the request. "Why do you need an identity card?" they ask. "Where do you plan to go? What do you plan to do?"

While I was in Niger, I thought sometimes of "Baba of Karo," an oral history recorded in 1949 by the British anthropologist Mary Smith. She spent weeks in the field listening to Baba, an old Muslim Hausa woman of northern Nigeria. Her story, the observations of her life as Smith transcribed them, is startlingly matter-of-fact. "Boys follow their fathers," Baba says. "They learn to farm and recite the Koran; girls follow their mothers, they spin and cook." And this, "My mother was a secluded wife, she didn't leave the compound."[2]

Baba's story came to mind one day at a checkpoint near Niamey, where I watched a very young gendarme, a machine gun slung over his shoulder, snap his fingers at an old woman, stooped and wrinkled, sitting in front of me in a minibus. He wanted her identity card. She sat still, staring at the floor, hands in her lap. The gendarme grabbed her high on her arm, yanking her easily from her seat and out the side door. He said, "Where is your baggage?" She had only a small plastic bag. The driver and two older men pleaded with the gendarme in low tones, addressing him as *patron.*

"She is old, *patron*," said one man. "What do you gain from doing this?"

"*Patron*," said another man, "let her be on her way, please."

The gendarme enjoyed this attention. It confirmed his power. He reclined in a steel lawn chair beneath a tree, munching on peanuts and paying half attention to the men's words. After an hour he let the old woman back on the bus. The passengers, including the driver and the two men, ignored her the rest of the trip.

I recall as well a scene from Mali years before. On the Niger River, outside the city of Gao, I had paid a boy to take me in his canoe the half mile across the slow-moving chocolate mass to the road where I hoped to hitchhike south to Bamako, Mali's capital. At the road head on the far bank, I waited at a checkpoint, sipping coffee at a food table beside a guard hut made of millet stalks.

The coffee man burst out laughing, pointing at a couple emerging from the hut—a stout woman and a soldier, she a little taller than he. The woman stumbled, laughing with the back of her hand over her mouth, as the soldier rushed behind yelling: "*Il faut me respecter, il faut me respecter!*" Then he kicked her in the rear. She went down.

The woman—perhaps two hundred pounds and five feet ten inches tall, wearing a flower-patterned multicolor wraparound cloth—lay sprawled on her stomach in the loose, wet sand at the roadside. She was laughing uncontrollably, a staccato, high-pitched sound punctuated by deep, gasping breaths. The soldier, short and thin like a fence post, wearing faded fatigues and black beret, stood over her, his rage equal to her mirth.

"*IImm-bée-cii-lle!*" he roared with French emphasis on the syllables, his arms at his sides. The woman rose on her hands and knees, giggling; wet sand dropped from her front in small clumps. But the soldier again applied the toe of his black leather boot to the center of her behind, sending the woman's arms out so her torso landed with a thud that expelled the air from her chest in a loud grunt. "Ooooomf!" She uttered no protest, betrayed no pain.

"You insult me," shouted the soldier, hands on hips. The woman stayed put, wordless, propping her elbows in the sand to rest her head in the palms of her hands. Her eyes looked skyward, bored. Lethal contempt. The soldier, scowling behind a splotchy beard, stomped off to his hut and drew a pink curtain across the entrance. She rose calmly and brushed off the sand, smoothing out the wrinkles in the wet, sand-stained cloth with both hands. She walked away with short, determined strides to the northwest along the river's edge.

The morning after the thief's beating, I found Hajia Mariatou in her office at 8:00 A.M. She looked up at me from the table where she sat working on her books and barely smiled when I clapped softly outside the open door. Her energy had returned, but Mariatou was serious and preoccupied. Silently, she continued working. I took a seat and examined a driver's manual. After a while, she said, "I'm going to the police station. Do you want to come?" She had to file a report about the thief, but she told me she really hoped to learn what had happened to him. The entire affair, the beating and the possibility that he might be dead, had traumatized her. "Everyone knows me in this city," she said. "That's why the thief was caught and beaten like that. I fear they killed him. That's not right." She paused and sighed. She continued softly. "But the police, I don't like dealing with them."

At Niamey's Central Police Commissariat, Mariatou proved her notoriety, moving through the compound as if campaigning, which she was in a way, acknowledging policemen who greeted her warmly by name and asked after her husband, her children, her work. She kept her answers and greetings brief. Her power was in her ability to do this alone, unaccompanied by a man (as a foreigner, I was of no consequence), although normally a man's presence is required to validate a woman's identity. In Niger, a woman is like the dependent clause of a complex sentence—incomprehensible and unreliable if left alone. Mariatou kept her head bowed, eyes to the ground, when she spoke to these men, who liked to call her "Madame Chauffeur" or "Hajia Chauffeur." I had begun to recognize Mariatou's power, her talent for survival. She knew when to assert herself and make her feelings known, and she knew when to wait. She sensed when she could afford to push against her world. What I found unusual was that she pushed at all.

Without appointment or delay, an inspector in a blue cotton tunic and trousers received her, addressing her properly as "Hajia." I might have waited hours for such attention. He offered her a chair, ignoring me, and sat at his desk below a picture of the army commander. Mariatou's polite smile turned cold. She answered questions in good

French, hands folded in her lap. In public, African women avoid eye contact with men, and, accordingly, Mariatou focused on the inspector's desk as he took her statement. He moved his gaze back and forth between her face and his notepad.

"No, I've never seen the man before," she told him. "No, this has never happened to me before." Then: "I'm not sure who saw him try to steal the car. A boy just came to tell me they had caught someone trying to steal it, and when I went out they were beating the man." The inspector nodded and murmured.

Mariatou sat quietly as the man made notes. Then she said, "Inspector, I want to know what happened to the thief. Is he alive?"

He put up a hand, a plea for patience as he continued writing. "Yes, Madame, yes. One moment."

"Is he alive?" Silence. "Inspector—"

"A moment, Madame, please." I could not help but think this was his way to remind Mariatou of his authority. The inspector controlled the dialogue. He made notes. He made her wait.

The inspector put down his pen. He sighed and looked out the window several seconds. "Madame Hajia, the man was in a very bad way when they brought him in, not even seeming to breathe, I am told. I didn't inquire further about the matter, but I know he's not being held here now. I don't know where he is."

Mariatou was calm, though I was acutely aware of my own nervousness, fed by the notion that no woman or man casually challenges an African police inspector or questions him on anything. I imagined that soon there would be some abrupt interference in her husband's business, a sudden finding that he or Mariatou was in violation of an obscure law. I imagined arrests in the night, the seizure of the driving school.

Mariatou stared a few moments at the inspector's chest. Then she said, abruptly, "*Merci, Monsieur.*"

Some in Niger believe that in the early spring of 1899, a woman (some say she was Hausa and others say Fulani), a sorceress queen who lived in southwestern Niger, fatally weakened Captain Voulet's renegade military expedition. The facts of this woman's story are elusive. She is known, for instance, only by the Hausa word for queen, *sarraounia*. There are bits of legend passed down. More substantially, there are the records of Captain Voulet and the journals of other officers involved in the affair. The French journalist Jacques-Francis Rolland, in *Le grand capitaine*, quotes Voulet, whose ambitions were blunted by heat, water shortages, and harsh winds: "It's Sarraounia," the captain tells his officers. "She's wishing us welcome."[3]

I'm not an anthropologist. I don't understand the full extent of male-female relationships in Africa, or anywhere else. But I suspect the legend of Sarraounia may explain why men in Africa work so hard to keep women subordinate. They fear women.

Sarraounia ruled in the region of Dogondoutchi. She reportedly had spiritual powers and may or may not have been in the habit of sleeping with the most handsome men of her realm, and then beheading them. Queen Amina of Katsina, who ruled to the south in British Nigeria, had the same fetish. But the African soldiers in Captain Voulet's command blamed their nightmares on Sarraounia. There is, for example, this entry in the journal of Lieutenant Meynier, one of the officers sent to arrest Voulet. The entry is dated June 20, 1899, in Matankari, a village in the Dogondoutchi region. "There fell upon us in this village a strange event. . . . In the middle of the night, the entire camp was awakened by hideous screams. A soldier was in the middle of a horrible dream and it was extremely difficult to wake him. He said, then, in his dream he had seen our detachment attacked and cruelly decimated by friendly soldiers."[4]

Little is known about Sarraounia. But this much is verifiable. Sarraounia mounted a brief, unsuccessful resistance against Voulet;

she was never captured. Later, the soldier's dream prophecy seemed to be fulfilled when Voulet attacked his French pursuers and then died himself at the hands of his own soldiers.

Some argue, however—including Niger's best-known writer, the late Abdoulaye Mamani—that the African soldiers may have been manipulated by Sarraounia's magic; it infected their minds and turned them against each other. In his novel *Sarraounia*, published in France in 1983, Mamani speculates on a selfless heroine, a female model for Pan-African independence and power, and a model for leadership. "This woman knew how to preserve her kingdom, by the sword and by magic against all who would subjugate and humiliate her."[5]

There is, I believe, imbedded in this tangle of legend and history, something more sinister, an unintentional implication. The idea that women must have superhuman powers to accomplish anything meaningful. And veiled beneath this, in the nether world of loose historical speculation that whirls around this story, is the suggestion of inherent evil and betrayal, scorpionlike, threatening to break the surface of female character—the predatory woman creature, Sarraounia or Queen Amina or whomever, capable of sexual intimacy, political genius, strength in battle, bearing children, and killing her lover all at once.

Mariatou gave me Hajia Ladi's address with these words. "I don't know her well, but I have met her. She is a courageous woman." Now, in Zinder, six hundred miles east of Niamey on the national highway, I was sitting with Ladi, sixty-four years old, a trader whose ambitions got her in trouble. She was telling me, as she fingered the papers in her hands, how she had lost money on the minibus she had bought seven years before. "I could not trust my drivers. I'd hire one and fire him, and then another." She insisted on holding drivers and soldiers accountable. Ladi challenged drivers to show receipts for the passengers they took and asked soldiers to explain the "fines" they imposed. Radical steps on the African road. Most transporters who are not also drivers negotiate a "fee" with checkpoint gendarmes, but Ladi simply refused to pay.

Hajia Ladi sat the way she preferred, atop pillows on a straw mat, while I leaned forward in a white steel lawn chair in the sandy compound of her home, shaded by high mud walls. We spoke French with the help of her teenage grandson, a lycée student who translated into Hausa what she could not understand of my French.

This is what makes Hajia Ladi important: She has never been a driver, but she is one of the first women in Niger to own commercial vehicles. She is the model, however imperfect, for Mariatou's dream of a bush taxi line. Ladi has eight children. Her first husband died; her second husband, a cloth trader, left seven years ago to find work in Cameroon and has not been heard from since. Ladi walks with a cane, having never fully recovered from an accident in her minibus bush taxi six years before. What she had to say of her experience was like the stories of most transporters, until she talked about her legs. The left leg is okay, but her right leg is stiff. She sat—a heavy woman in bright cotton wraps—with that leg, the skin of her bare ankle chapped and scaled, extended straight out like a fallen log.

Ladi showed me evidence of her past. Her grandson brought her a dusty red vinyl briefcase, its handle broken. She set it on her lap, flipped the latch, and opened the case. She carefully ruffled through receipts, registration papers, carbon copies of police reports, a driver's logbook in a plastic folder, and yellowing photographs, all of it stuffed and folded into that square space. "Ah, here," she said, handing me a wrinkled photo of a Toyota minibus, which was still parked outside her compound, the tires flat. There were photos, too, of a Renault city taxi she owned fifteen years before; it broke down after a year on the road. And of a Peugeot 404 station wagon she bought five years later to transport vegetables back and forth between Zinder and Kano, Nigeria. That venture lasted a year. She shook her head. "The soldiers wanted money or they took vegetables. Always something. I sold the Peugeot and bought the bus to carry people." That was her last gamble in the transport business. When I spoke to her, Ladi was living off her extended family and some vegetable trading from family gardens.

"After a few months, I chose to ride every trip to count the passengers they [the drivers] took, and the money," she said. "Otherwise they would take more money than they were allowed and lie about the numbers of passengers. And the drivers would never argue enough with the soldiers. I'm not afraid to do that." She shook her finger at me as she spoke and then laughed ironically. Ladi's humor, her lack of overt bitterness, caught my attention. She dealt with crisis, I imagined, through the fatalism of Islam, surrendering her life to Allah's will. Or was it a sense of defeat? This woman had tried to control her fate, unsuccessfully, by monitoring her drivers and challenging gendarmes, by carving out a transport business of her own, and losing it.

One night, on Route 1 somewhere not far west of Zinder, her driver, a man she had hired a month earlier, hit a cow. The minibus sideswiped the beast's head on the front passenger side, where Ladi was sitting. "I was thrown against the windshield," she said, "and my legs got badly bruised." She patted her right leg. "This one, I really don't know what happened with it." Ladi spent days in the Zinder hospital and was even treated, she said, by a French doctor. In the end, the gendarmes charged her and the driver with reckless driving, and she, not the driver, paid the heavy fine (it came to about one hundred dollars) plus much more to repair the bus. But, she added, "I know the driver did it on purpose to ruin my business. I saw how he drove straight for the cow and he was not hurt." Neither were any passengers.

She paused and looked at me. "And I know the driver split my fine with the soldiers. They all took the money. That's just how it is."

Mariatou was close to giving up on finding the thief. "I think he is dead, but I want to be sure," she said. "If he's alive, he needs help. But the police will never say anything about this matter."

She told me this as she drove the Peugeot, the alleged thief's object of desire, back to the UNICEF office. We had spent the afternoon picking up and delivering documents—letters to the post office, sealed envelopes to the French embassy and the offices of CARE International, a stack of reports to the Ministry of Health, where it took Mariatou twenty minutes just to get through the lobby as she greeted and exchanged pleasantries with secretaries, nurses, soldiers, administrators.

Back in the Peugeot, we turned off the Boulevard Charles de Gaulle (one of the city's few paved roads) near the French consulate, on to the Boulevard Martin Luther King. Mariatou quickly hit forty miles an hour on this narrow road that skirts Niamey's Plateau district, the residential area for diplomats and foreign missions. Mariatou did not seem to notice her speed.

"We never saw the body after they took it away," I said in an attempt to be reassuring. "You can never be sure what happened to him." The police, so far, had not harassed Mariatou or her husband. She had sent inquiries to the police inspector, but he had not replied.

"Aren't you afraid your questions will cause trouble for you with the police?" I asked.

She shrugged. "Why? How? What would they do?"

In the next moment, though, Mariatou seemed to second-guess her own self-assurance. She shook her head, braking hard and then gently as we approached a T-intersection. "I'm not going back to the inspector to find out for sure." I didn't feel like asking her why.

At the T, near the city's secondary school inspectorate, Mariatou turned left. "I know almost everyone at the market. If he were alive, somehow I would find out. I'd have heard by now." She sighed. "He must be dead." Through Plateau, Niamey's only neighborhood with paved streets, she made a series of left and right turns past large bungalows. Then Mariatou looked at me and, for the first time, asked me a question.

"He is dead, don't you think?"

Road Journal

NIAMEY, JUNE 9, 1993. I feel schizophrenic. I waver between moral outrage—in the presence of gendarmes, bureaucrats, and certain drivers—and respect and admiration for people like Issoufou Garba, Hajia Mariatou, and Keletigui Mariko. Sometimes I'm in awe of them. My thoughts move from intense selfishness—the desire to get the hell out of this place just to save my own small life—and the feeling that I must spend a few more months with Issoufou, who will be here for the rest of his life. My head is filled with anger, fear, and guilt, especially guilt that I have used Issoufou. When I saw him in Zinder during my trip with Mariko, I didn't have a good feeling about him. Issoufou didn't have his usual energy.

The outrage is winning the battle in my head. Outrage and fear. I want out of this place. Maybe there is no spiritual belief here, no real respect for the road. Maybe there is only wanton disregard, contempt, anger, disrespect. A grand selfishness. Maybe selfishness is the only effective tool for survival here. In my most bitter moments I think the road and everyone on it is the enemy and should be treated as one treats a vicious dog on the street: Don't dare show fear. Don't make eye contact. Just go straight on ahead as if this is your own territory, as if nothing is wrong. That way, you might have a chance to survive. On some level, though, you become one of the vicious dogs. On a street here in Niamey yesterday, I had to work very hard to keep from mouthing off to a policeman who, on a whim, demanded my passport.

> A patient man can melt a rock.
> — Hausa proverb

An Ugly American

The first *gri-gri* disappeared in May, before my brief last visit to Zinder. It fell through a hole in a side pocket of my shoulder bag. Soon afterward, I lost the second one off a cord around my neck. I am not sure how or where or when. Muggers took my third and last amulet on a dark street late on a June evening in Niamey. On my way back from drinking with friends at a bar, I felt someone put his arm around my neck and pull me to the ground, while another person yanked the bag so the shoulder strap snapped before I reached the concrete. I had heard nothing of the thieves' approach, but I saw two shadowy figures run off the street into the wide, sandy gully of a public garden known to be a thieves' hideout. I scrambled to my feet screaming and pursued them into the trees and bushes. The thought of my passport and money in that bag drove me until I realized I was in darkness alone, unarmed, and unfamiliar with the terrain. All that took five minutes.

Back on the road I met an army patrol, four men who had been eating dinner on the roadside nearby when they heard my screams.

They stood there staring at me, one shirtless and the other three with green tunics unbuttoned. One was barefoot and the others wore sandals. They were breathing hard and carried automatic rifles. One asked, honestly concerned, "Are you all right, Monsieur?" I nodded, embarrassed at the attention, and at my stupidity. "You should know these streets are dangerous at night," another soldier said. "You are lucky they did not use a knife."

Together we spread out in search of the thieves. In a line, with me in the middle, we crouched low and stepped silently, weaving through the bush. The soldiers had fixed bayonets to their guns. One told me they feared ambush. I felt pathetic. I was sneaking around with these men hoping to recover a few dollars and a passport the U.S. embassy needed only a day to replace. I convinced the soldiers to give up. They walked me the few hundred yards to the house where I was staying. In gratitude, I offered them the remaining money in my pocket, two thousand francs. They politely refused my offer and walked away. The next day, or maybe the next week, at some checkpoint they might justify extortion to cover unpaid wages. But in me, perhaps, they had found a chance to act like the protectors they were supposed to be. A brief reason for being.

Later, what bothered me was losing the last of my *gris-gris*, taken as if only theft and violence would permit fate or the demons to reclaim the talisman before I flew off the continent. The absence of all three *gris-gris* made me slightly nervous. For months I had taken them for granted, their dim protective presence in the background of daily living in the shadow of the road. My relationship to these vague objects, their importance to me, became clearer when they were gone. Maybe I had failed to get the point that I was supposed to leave my *gris-gris* behind—not with Malam Shafi, who had given them to me, but somewhere along the road: in a mosque, a home, on the pavement. I don't know. I understood only in the end that they were on loan.

Issoufou Garba reminded me of this in anger. In June, a few weeks before I left Niger, I returned to Zinder. At Issoufou's home one evening, I told him about the mugging, leaving out my fear of traveling without the *gris-gris*. Annoyed, he brushed aside the story. *Of course* I had not been hurt, he said, and *of course* I had lost nothing of great value. The *gris-gris* had forever marked my life by saving it, but they had never belonged to me in the first place. They were on loan, he told me, and I should have known that.

"Issoufou, I didn't understand this."

"That doesn't matter," he said. He spoke coolly and would not look at me. "You cannot own *gris-gris*. Their value cannot be seen or held. *Gris-gris* cannot be completely understood." Malam Shafi had explained that. Indeed, I remembered.

Later, we were talking early one morning, sipping instant Nescafé from glasses at our coffee table outside the motor park. Issoufou was again lecturing me about the *gris-gris*, and he addressed a new theme: my general lack of responsibility as a visitor to his country. I was uncomfortable. He paused and shook his head. We were silent awhile. Business had not been good for months. Two of his three vehicles had broken down. He had no gas and he would not buy any until the moment he had secured enough passengers to go someplace. Issoufou traveled twice a week now if he was lucky. On this day he was unlucky.

"Transport is not working now," he said. Issoufou had said this several times in the five days I had been back. I wondered if his mood reflected anger with life or true disappointment—in me and in the fact that I was leaving at a particularly inauspicious time for him. Issoufou was failing.

He resumed his lesson. "It was very arrogant of you to think you could take the *gris-gris*. They served their purpose for you. Because of the *gris-gris*, the soldiers were there to save you. And you have never been in an accident. You are alive. You are healthy. The marabout did not intend them to be souvenirs." He spoke in a monotone, shaking his head again. "You have gotten what you came here for."

This was humiliating. I tried to continue our conversation.

"What will you do, Issoufou? Things will get better eventually, but what will you do until then?"

"I don't know. That's up to God. It's not your problem."

"Why don't you sell one of the cars? You could repair the other two, keep them running, feed your family."

He sighed. "I've been trying to sell. Even in Maradi, no one is buying anything right now." Then, shaking his head, he said, "*Ça ne va pas, ça ne va pas.*"

In the morning, Issoufou's was the only bush taxi waiting at the motor park to go to Maradi. Five people paid the fare, enough to justify a trip. He bought gasoline. At 9:00 A.M., steering wheel in one hand, he turned the ignition key with the other. *Click.* The engine did not turn over. He turned the key three more times, jerking it hard and gently pumping the gas pedal. We both knew he had been ignoring an ignition problem for months, but on the third click the engine caught and hummed normally. Issoufou maneuvered the car to the motor park gate, paid the policeman, and drove into the street. Same routine, though the park itself had changed. Many drivers had left to find work in Nigeria, Maradi, or Niamey, so the park, usually a scene of happy chaos any time of day, was strangely calm and mostly devoid of travelers. Even the *komasho* were gone.

After a few yards, the engine kicked and coughed. Issoufou pumped the gas pedal but couldn't increase his speed. The car rolled forward in soft jerking motions for a hundred yards before it died. He started the car again and traveled a few more yards before the engine quit a second time. Issoufou sat back, silent. Our passengers said nothing.

We were sitting in Issoufou's last and newest hope, his 1971 Peugeot station wagon, which he had bought months earlier. We were close to the motor park and a mechanic if the car could just make it the short distance back.

"It's the fuel filter or carburetor," Issoufou murmured. "Full of sand, I'm sure." He wanted to give the engine another chance, so we waited a few minutes. Perhaps the problem would work itself out. The car started again, but it died almost immediately. I suspected Issoufou was right in his diagnosis, having experienced this situation many times as a bush taxi passenger. The loss of power, the slow-fast indecision of a fuel-starved engine. In this land of dust and contaminated gasoline, fuel filters and carburetors are often the first to go.

Issoufou seemed nervous. He sat behind the wheel, clasping and unclasping his hands. I had returned to Zinder because I wanted to say good-bye to a friend, and because I wanted to get a sense of what would happen to Issoufou after I left. I wanted to be sure of where he was going with this line of work. And Issoufou, I had begun to understand, was trying to get a sense of where I was going with mine. At the coffee table that morning, he said that I hadn't spent enough time with him and in Niger. "You white people," he complained, not for the first time, "you come, you stay a bit, you gather your information or whatever you came for, and then you leave your projects." He had broken this argument to me two nights before while we drank tea in the compound of his home. "French, German, American, whatever, you come and you go, and what do you leave?" I couldn't argue with him, couldn't answer his question. His attitude was disturbingly bitter, unlike him, as if he were near to giving up. I had been trying to explain that my money was almost gone, that I'd definitely be back. I was struck, though, by the cliché sound of my claim, "I'll be back." My money really was nearly gone, but I also felt tired. Tired physically and tired of being scared. And I was feeling increasingly uncomfortable around Issoufou.

"You are right," I told him. "I haven't spent enough time. I will be back."

"When?"

"I don't know."

"You don't know. Ha!"

Issoufou knew what he was talking about. He was once the book-keeper for a European agricultural project. The researchers were trying to develop more fertile, easier-to-grow crop seedlings to secure stable food resources. Corn, sorghum, millet. The project failed, a victim, I gathered from what Issoufou told me, of its own expensive and grandiose ideas conceived in the minds of people familiar only with fertile terrain, not with drought-stricken Niger. They were Americans, Germans, Canadians. "None of them spoke French or Hausa," Issoufou said. In the end, the foreigners left.

So, aware that my own work would leave Issoufou with only a memory of me and the fare money I paid him, I was treading delicately. His two other Peugeots, lacking spare parts for repair, were parked on the street outside his house. The oldest car needed a new carburetor, the other, a new alternator and fan.

What Issoufou really needed was money. My powerlessness to help annoyed me. Many times I had been in trouble with Issoufou, broken down in Zinder or out on some isolated patch of road, and always we had come out all right. But this was different. Government salaries and student aid now went completely unpaid; check-point soldiers were taking more money than ever; the schools had been closed for months. Money was not circulating, and travelers were few. Issoufou had trouble paying for repairs. In January, during somewhat better times, I had offered to help him buy a new carburetor to replace the bad one on the oldest car. "I don't need your help," he told me.

Now, Issoufou slammed the steering wheel with the palms of both hands. "*Merde!*" He rested his forehead on his arms draped over the wheel. One passenger, a young man, laughed and shook his head. He said, loudly, "*Mais, bien sûr, c'est le Niger, mon beau pays.*"—Well, of course, this is Niger, my beautiful country. The young woman he was traveling with said, "Allah, Allah." Issoufou yanked the engine hood lever and opened his door to get out. A civil servant sitting in the far rear—he had said he wanted to get to Maradi "this morning"—sat and stared. An old man in the middle row massaged his face with both hands, groaning and mumbling through his fingers. "*Problèmes, problèmes, problèmes.*"

Issoufou, hunched over the engine, wasn't talking.

It was uncertain whether another bush taxi would leave for Maradi that day. The park was still empty of vehicles and it was now close to 9:00 A.M. The other men and I got out of the car, ready to push it off the road.

Then I heard what I'd been expecting to hear any moment. The young woman said, "*Chauffeur, donne moi mon argent.*"—Driver, give me my money.

An American relief worker I met in Niamey told me this in earnest: "Africans make the worst mechanics, the worst drivers, the worst car owners, and everyone knows that." My acquaintance insisted on the point. "They push their machines to the absolute edge and they don't bother to maintain them. There's no logic in what they do. It makes no sense." She paused as if finished, but then added, "I am not sympathetic. They can't maintain them. They don't know how. They don't even try."

There is, in that argument, anger and frustration, a good deal of justifiable fear, bad memories of long bush taxi rides, memories of wrecks witnessed and heard about, and a shred of truth.

Only a shred.

I didn't bother to assert a counterargument, but I considered inviting this person to visit a bush taxi garage I knew of in Niamey, situated on the edge of the Wadata motor park. My idea was to put things in perspective for her, but I thought better of it. The garage was typical, really just an open, dusty compound full of grease, flies, and loose metal, the useful pieces of which were piled neatly on oily cloths. Useless parts lay scattered in the dirt among twisted, hollowed-out wrecks; and there were a dozen pesky adolescent apprentice mechanics—teenage boys, some as young as ten—taking time out from their regular lives as street urchins. Every one of them was a cousin or brother or nephew of the mechanic who ran the place. Yet, that tangled stimulus would only feed my interlocutor's argument that irresponsibility governs African road transport. I decided against showing her the garage, and eventually dismissed her argument, preferring the shelter of my own judgment.

The images and details I found in Niger's garages and motor parks signaled genius and inspiration to me, ingenuity born of will and a talent for survival in a land of meager resources. In Niger, indeed, in all of Africa, a mechanic's method depends on intuition, creativity, experimentation, and patience. One might say the same about mechanics anywhere, but in developing countries it means something very different. The mechanic in Niger, if he is to survive, has little choice but to be creative. He must train himself, must work with what knowledge, tools, and materials he has. He must make it up as he goes along.

An image for thought: In Zinder's ancient Birni quarter, a twenty-three-year-old Nigerien mechanic named Moussa Albert has inherited a project and livelihood from his uncle, a government mechanic who trained Moussa on his own vehicle—a 1948 Dodge Power Wagon pickup. The old mechanic is dead now, and no one remembers where he got the truck. People do remember how awful it looked and ran when he began to rebuild it with his protégé, Moussa, who grew up around that machine. He was fifteen when his uncle offered to make a mechanic of him. Together, they stripped the decayed auto body and rebuilt it with sheet metal from the wreck of a semi. They welded the metal to the chassis so the truck resembled a World War I vintage tank without a top. They installed a used Toyota Land Cruiser engine that came from a retired government truck. They reshaped the old Dodge's engine cavity with hammers and welding tools so the Toyota engine would fit, like a transplanted heart. The project took three years. When the truck was finished in 1990, months before Moussa's uncle died, they painted the machine bright yellow. Moussa also painted, in red block letters, the name *Super Coptérre* on the truck's two doors. He got the name from the French title of an American action film starring a high-tech helicopter. Moussa now hauls people, kola nuts, mail, foodstuffs, and whatever else he can between Zinder and villages in the deep, roadless bush, places where his vehicle with its huge tractor tires and indestructible body can easily go. He has a near monopoly on the bush taxi transport market between Zinder and the Nigerian border, fifty-four miles to the south.

After forty-five years, that Dodge Power Wagon is still on the road near the edge of a new millennium. Car enthusiasts around the world buy all sorts of old car models and perform similar mechanical feats in their spare time. They are hobbyists with deeper resource pools. The *Super Coptérre*, on the other hand, is something far more special, an example of adaptation and survival in Africa.

Let me tell you more about mechanics in Niger. They are not like shoes, as you might describe mechanics in the United States, where you can actually try one on, and then another, and maybe another until you find "your" mechanic, the one that fits, the one you trust. Many of us become upset when our mechanic moves away. Some people follow a mechanic who changes garages. On the other hand, other car owners, mystified and unnerved by what goes on under the engine hood, nervously settle for any mechanic. An affordable point of view in the United States, a land of comparatively limitless resources, what the Hausa call *kaya dayowa*—many things, the knick-knacks of wealth. We can afford to be fickle, to be choosy or not. We trade in a car with only seventy thousand miles on it. In Niger, people told me, "*Kuna da kaya dayowa cikin Amerique.*"—You have many things in America. Abundant new spare parts, dashboard CD players and navigating devices, auto factories, mechanic schools, and computers that troubleshoot engine problems when the mechanic's knowledge fails him. Time. Money. Material.

In Niger, you put your faith in whatever mechanic you find, in whatever spare part might do the job. If you've been driving awhile, you get to know good mechanics and bad ones, like anywhere, but in Niger there are few to choose from. The very good ones tend to be already employed with the government or the relief agencies.

Issoufou's mechanic was a man he called *le bandit*, a Nigerian who had resettled in Niger from Onitsha, a city in southeastern Nigeria. His name was Oliver and we had relied on him many times. He had a "garage" near the motor park. But before Issoufou could walk off to find him, the passengers wanted their money. I stood behind this scene so Issoufou could not see me. Watching him hand back his profits was painful. A few minutes later, the old man and the civil servant helped me push the car off the road. Then they left.

Issoufou went to find *le bandit*. He returned with him after a few minutes. Oliver walked up with his hands in the pockets of dirty khaki trousers. He was about thirty, tall, lean, and muscular in a greasy purple T-shirt. This was the third time I had met him. In good English, he said, "You have come back. I thought you had the sense to leave this place."

Oliver suggested, in poor Hausa, that we roll the car down the road to his home, where he worked. We had to push the Peugeot a hundred yards to a gap in the median where we could turn it around.

The job would be easy on a flat street. Oliver and I positioned ourselves in the rear and pushed while Issoufou leaned in to steer from the driver's side, right hand on the steering wheel, the other atop the open door.

Issoufou and I were standing on opposite sides of the engine. From the front end, leaning over the radiator, *le bandit* put his screwdriver and wrench in his pocket (they were the only tools I saw him use) and, with both hands, gently lifted the carburetor off the engine. He held it up to the sunlight for better exposure, peering into the fuel chamber. He squinted and carefully turned the object over in his hands, holding it close to his face. In English—for my benefit—he announced what we could clearly see. "It's very dirty." Grit was caked in the carburetor's surface grooves. Oliver lowered the carburetor to his chest and walked to a metal table beneath a neem tree in the corner of his compound. There, he dunked it in a small plastic bucket of gasoline on the ground. "Clean gasoline," he told us. He smiled at me, swirling the carburetor in the liquid to loosen the dirt. "I buy mine from only the best smugglers." He paused, looked at Issoufou, and playfully shook the handle of his screwdriver at him. In broken French, he said, "I used to buy from him."

Issoufou, enjoying this and seeing the playful implication in his friend's gesture, pointed at him and looked at me, smiling. Issoufou said, "*Lui là, il est grand voleur—fait attention.*"—That man there, is a great thief—be careful. Then, to Oliver, a reminder: "*Kai, Bandit!* Remember, that's my carburetor you have there." He announced this with mock seriousness. Issoufou and I had been through this sort of banter before with mechanics, *komasho*, parts vendors, drivers, gendarmes. I understood the routine to be good-natured ribbing that carried a veiled warning—"Don't rip me off."

But we had always done well with Oliver. He laughed at Issoufou's words as he carefully swirled the carburetor around in the gasoline.

I once asked him where he learned his trade. He said, "I went through secondary school and a mechanic's training program the British set up, but life is so difficult in Nigeria. Too many people, too many mechanics, and politics in Nigeria, Oooohhhh." His voice trailed off and he shook his head. "I make a better living here." Oliver liked to talk.

In Oliver's compound, a single square mud building squatted on one end. He lived alone. A small, gray metal classroom chair lay overturned in the dirt beside the open front door. The only other home furnishing, a dirty foam mattress, lay folded up on a straw mat just inside the entrance. Oliver's work dominated the compound. Under the broad shade of a tree in one corner stood the table where he performed intricate tasks. He had no electricity, no hydraulic lift, no machine tools, no running water. He kept tools and important spare parts in two large metal boxes. After a while I noticed the boxes were really battered old refrigerators set on their backs against the mud wall that enclosed the compound. "The army was throwing them away," he told me, "so I took them." He kept the boxes padlocked.

I liked Oliver. I admired his resourcefulness, his humor and endurance. As he waited for the gasoline to work on the carburetor, he spoke in broken French and Hausa, and occasionally English, while juggling, quite expertly, three heavy lug nuts. "Our teacher taught us this in secondary school," he said. The act delighted Issoufou, who took a seat on the ground with his back against the tree and watched. "*Kai!*" Issoufou said, grinning his approval. Issoufou's mood change was a relief, however brief. I asked Oliver to tell me more about his mechanic's training.

"I used to work at the Peugeot plant in Kaduna," Oliver said, his eyes following the lug nuts. "The assembly line, you know. Hours a day putting on wheels, nothing but wheels. Then, after a few weeks I was putting in seats, after that, shocks. I learned some things, but a mechanic cannot grow on the assembly line. Too much repetition." One of the nuts fell and he bent to pick it up. He set all three together on the table. "Now, here I am. I have my own garage in a country where nothing works and no one can pay me." He laughed at this and then added in French, "*Mais, c'est l'Afrique.*" Then, suddenly serious, Oliver said, "But life is calmer in Niger." I thought of the irony: the political and social chaos Nigeria's oil wealth has bought as opposed to the relative stability poverty has brought to Niger, even with a disorderly government transition.

Oliver grinned at me and raised a finger. "You know, they say you should never trust a Nigerian. We are all supposed to be drug dealers." He laughed at this. "Every time I travel in this country, the police give me so many problems."

I said, "They give us all problems." I nodded at Issoufou. "Just talk to him." Oliver spoke the truth, though. Beyond close examination of my papers, gendarmes rarely caused me serious trouble—a result, I liked to think, of my *gris-gris*—but gendarmes were merciless with their own citizens and anyone from another African country. I had found this to be true not just in Niger, but anywhere I went in West Africa. For me, arbitrary arrest had become part of the road's permanent background.

Oliver's repair work did not end with the carburetor. He removed part of the fuel system's plastic tubing, sharply blowing through the tube ends to clear the fuel lines of sand. He took out and checked the fuel filter, which was also gritty with sand. Oliver rotated the filter in front of his eyes, squinting again, with his fingers moving on opposite ends of the plastic cylinder. He put it on the table and opened one of the toolboxes to look for a used filter that might work.

The last thing to do was clean out the carburetor, which Oliver now began to do, having removed it from the bucket and put it on an oily old cloth atop the table. With his fingers, a screwdriver, occasionally his tongue, he scraped out little chunks of sand from inside the cavity and from the grooved outer surfaces, dipping the carburetor now and then back into the bucket's grainy pink fluid.

Oliver smiled at us and explained, again for my benefit, what was obvious to Issoufou. "Bad petrol. Lots of sand." Contaminated contraband gasoline sand. Nigerian sand. Lifting the carburetor from the bucket, he wiped it off with a cloth and put his mouth to the fuel chamber. Puckering like a trumpeter, he blew into it three times before returning it to the bucket and repeating the process.

Finished, Oliver turned his head to wipe his lips on the shoulder of his T-shirt and rubbed his hands on a cloth hanging from a nail in the tree. He repeated his findings, this time in French. "*C'est l'essence qui fait ça*"—The gas does this—he said to Issoufou, "*toujours l'essence du Nigeria*"—always Nigerian gasoline. My friend, still sitting against the tree, folded his arms and frowned. This fact was not going to cure Issoufou's petrol buying habits—the Nigerian stuff was ready and cheap—but it might make him more careful about inspecting its purity. A delicate matter with smugglers, who are a more volatile and dangerous group than even the *komasho*. They don't like to have their integrity or livelihood challenged. A few months before, when Nigerien customs officers made a serious effort to seize contraband Nigerian gasoline, smugglers marched on customs stations at border checkpoints and burned them. Issoufou knew that. And he knew that dirty fuel had cost him a day's profit.

Oliver looked at me. "How much would this job cost in your country?"

I shrugged. I actually didn't know. A few dollars for a new filter and labor costs for installation, and then the carburetor work. "Eighty dollars?" I said. "I'm guessing."

Oliver pursed his lips and was silent awhile. Finally he said, "Let's not talk about money." He wanted to talk more about Nigeria. "In Kaduna and Kano there are clandestine factories where people make fake Peugeot parts," he said. "And sometimes they just take old parts and make them look new so they will sell." He set the carburetor on the table. "I know these things. I used to work in one of those places.

I remade carburetors from used ones, just cleaned them up; and brake drums, too. But they didn't really work. You have to be very careful when you are picking over parts."

After a couple of hours the car was running fine. Issoufou slapped five hundred francs in Oliver's hands. The mechanic had earned about a buck seventy for two and a quarter hours of work. The rest was on credit, African credit: money when Oliver really needed it, or free transport, maybe food. This the two men understood implicitly. Here, currency comes in many forms.

There was one more problem, and Issoufou, knowing that I understood Oliver better than he did, asked me to translate. I was relieved that I could serve a purpose for my friend, even if momentary. There was a loud rattle in the car, Issoufou said, somewhere around the left front wheel. I had forgotten about this. Above fifty miles an hour the car's entire frame shook and squeaked in a cacophony of rattles and squeaks. The ignition problem, which struck me as more pressing, would have to wait. Issoufou, like any car owner, prioritized the repairs by what he could pay for and what seemed to him most serious. His decisions didn't always make sense to me. Among bush taxi drivers, car repair work tends to focus under the engine hood and on anything connected to the wheels. The rest is irrelevant. So, this particular sound worried Issoufou.

Consider the Peugeot's basic condition. Issoufou had tied the battery in place with rope that wrapped around part of the engine cavity's underframe and around the radiator. A thick wad of rag plugged the oil tank. Air and water hoses showed half a dozen patch jobs where aluminum strips (cut from Coke cans) had been glued and tightly wound around leaks. The door locks didn't work. Bare steel nodules stuck out where window handles should have been. Issoufou kept the only handle crank in his pocket, giving it out whenever someone wanted a window open or closed. The passenger would fasten the crank, work the window, and hand the crank back. Issoufou had sewn shut, using thick cord, a three-inch tear in the right front tire. The speedometer, temperature, and fuel gauges didn't work. The gauges had nothing directly to do with making the wheels turn, so they mattered little. When deciding what to repair, Issoufou practiced his own triage.

"Issoufou," I explained to Oliver, "is afraid of the sound because it might mean the wheel will fall off on the road."

We test-drove the car around the neighborhood so Oliver could hear the rattle. He blamed a shock absorber. Back in his compound, he removed the shock unit (a single cone-shaped component consisting of a thick steel spring wound around a hydraulic piston fastened to the axle) from behind and above the front left wheel. He discovered some loose screws that explained the rattle, and a worn shock pad. This flat, round piece of rubber, which fits on top of the spring, had deteriorated and come loose. With a new part, the repairs would be easy. The real challenge was finding the part, and that would be Issoufou's job.

"You have to be careful," Oliver warned us. "Be sure what you find is a Peugeot part, not something made of any old material." So, in the same car, with the shock absorber and old pad back in, we rattled this way and that across Zinder. We visited used parts shops, mechanics, roadside parts sellers, looking for something that looked like it might work. Issoufou was silent and irritable. We were eating up gas, time, and Issoufou's money, and I was waiting for the ignition to finally go out, a tire to go flat. Bush taxis run quite literally on hope; Issoufou's fair share appeared to have run out. The easy solution would have been to visit Zinder's one Peugeot franchise parts dealer, but Issoufou would not pay for a new shock pad. He knew the used parts vendors, so they let us take pads back to test them before paying.

Oliver was not pleased with what we had found. "This won't work, wrong model. No, not the right material. Take it back, too large. No, no, no," he said, waving us away. He had standards to maintain. I know little about engine maintenance, and Issoufou knew only the basics, which put him, like so many car owners, in the hands of his mechanic. He'd never seen a shock pad before, had never even considered its existence.

Neither had I.

The reality was frustrating, focused on the marketplace, in buyer competition, supply and demand. Zinder's only fully stocked and equipped garage belonged to the army garrison, which drew its supplies from the French military by cooperative agreement. The agreement included one full-time French mechanic, who maintained the garrison's several trucks and single tank, one of two owned by the Nigerien Army. Everyone else: the local government hospital with its two broken-down white Toyota ambulances, the regional forestry bureau and its one Toyota Land Cruiser, the Zinder police, and the Brigade Routière with their four aging blue Land Rovers—every government agency, every businessman, every bush taxi and car owner in the city, maybe 150 vehicles altogether—had to forage for used parts, looking for anything that was remotely functional. Most used parts were useless, hopelessly broken and worn. Old shock springs lay among piles of threadbare timing belts, broken distributor caps, a piece of carburetor, a rusted alternator. The few good parts sold quickly, and Oliver would not touch the stuff that remained. We found an abundance of decent parts for the rare Mercedes or Ford, but nothing for us. Keeping a car on the road in Africa is highly competitive work.

"You see what is happening?" Issoufou asked as we drove to another dealer. He was angry, and I let him run on. In this mood, he did not shout. He lectured, and I never argued with him. "You Europeans dump all your old cars on us," he said. "Even your clothes, all those shirts and pants and things you see in the market; people think they come from dead people in America and Europe. This is how you treat us. We can't even afford what new parts there are. It's the usual politics, the usual racism. We get what you don't want anymore."

Trying to rationalize, I began to tell Issoufou that the clothes are secondhand, not necessarily from dead people. Then, too late, I caught myself. He looked at me for a moment, his face blank, and then shook his head. "Secondhand," he said. "What's the difference? The insult is still there."

I was stung by the stupidity of my own words. "I'm sorry about this, Issoufou. What can I say?"

"Say nothing," Issoufou said. Later he said, "You know, I think you are bringing me bad luck."

Late in the afternoon Issoufou decided to buy a new shock pad from the regular Peugeot parts dealer. It cost him fifteen hundred francs, a thousand francs more than he had wanted to pay. "What choice is there?" he said. "Things are just not working right now."

I didn't attempt to help him with money, though I badly wanted to, and to tell him as well that this was no time for foolish pride. Later, it occurred to me that neither was it the time to believe money would make a bit of difference. For that moment, though, I so wanted to replace the shock pad, the carburetor, the tire with the sewn-up tear—to ease my conscience. I wanted us to part on good terms, but Issoufou just wanted me gone. In silence, we drove back to the motor park and Issoufou parked the Peugeot outside the union office where I had first met him. We got out of the car and he walked briskly away in the direction of his home.

I watched him go and did not follow. That night I went to Issoufou's home, but he would not see me. One of his wives spoke with me at the compound door. She smiled. "Issoufou is busy," she said in French. I heard men on the patio playing cards. There was gleeful shouting and someone, not Issoufou, was slapping cards down one by one. I told his wife I would wait. After a while Issoufou came outside.

We stood together for a few moments in the darkness, saying nothing. Then he said, "I have to stop driving for a while. There's no more reason for you to be here."

"I know. I want to thank you, Issoufou." I wanted to say much more—about the *gris-gris*, about money, about gratitude. I wanted to try and explain so many things, but it would all have come stumbling out of my mouth incoherently. "Thank you for everything you have done," I said again.

For the first time since I had been back in Zinder he smiled at me. "We'll see each other again some time."

"I hope so," I said. "I'm sure of it. I told you I'll be back." There were no more words. We shook hands and I walked away.

The next day, a Tuesday, I went to the motor park at dawn, hoping to find transport to Maradi, where I could get a car to Niamey. I waited all day. The union office was closed and Issoufou's car was gone. I sat on my bag in the shade of a large old bus, drinking tea and munching peanuts. I said a few good-byes and hugged a couple of drivers I knew. Oliver came to shake my hand and give me a letter for a Nigerian friend of his in Niamey.

The motor park was eerily quiet. A few vendors walked about. A boy carried a tray of stale cooked goat meat atop his head; a little girl sold peanuts in small plastic baggies. I bought two. One 504 station wagon and a minibus waited for Maradi passengers. I had been back in Zinder for a week. Now, on my way out and with only a few familiar faces around me, the park's blank emptiness struck with the pain of abandonment.

I waited.

No one had seen Issoufou that day. At 4:00 P.M. enough passengers had shown up to fill the 504. The driver was a stranger to me. I paid him for a cramped seat in the far rear. He looked up at me when I handed over my money. "Toureest," he said.

Notes

THE FICKLE GOD

1. Ben Okri, *The Famished Road* (London: Safari Books, 1992), 121.

2. From "Seven Pregnant Women Roasted to Death," *Prime People* (Lagos, Nigeria), March 4, 1993.

3. Graham Greene, *The Power and the Glory* (New York: Penguin Books, 1982), 25.

4. Graham Greene, *Journey without Maps* (Middlesex, England: Penguin Books, 1971), 1.

5. Automobile statistics for Africa and related data were compiled from the *1995 World Almanac*; a World Bank report entitled "The Road Maintenance Initiative," by Steve Carapetis, Hernan Levy, and Terje Wolden (Washington, D.C.: World Bank Economic Development Institute, 1991); and *World Transport Data*, published annually by the International Road Transport Union in Washington, D.C.

6. Hernan Levy and Patrick Malone, "Transport Policy Issues in Sub-Saharan Africa," EDI Policy Seminar Report 9 (Washington, D.C.: World Bank Economic Development Institute, 1988), 1.

THE DOGS OF THE ROAD

1. Heinrich Barth's account of a dust storm is from volume 3 of his memoir *Travels and Discoveries in North and Central Africa* (London: Frank Cass, 1965), 179.

2. Quotation from Captain Granderye, the first French officer to confirm Voulet's atrocities. Granderye, commandant of the French Niger River outpost at Say, detailed his observations in a routine political report dated March 1, 1899, for the French governor-general in Dakar. His reports are in the Central African Mission file at Niger's Archives Nationale in Niamey.

3. Levy and Malone, "Transport Policy Issues in Sub-Saharan Africa," 2.

A DRIVER, A CHECKPOINT, AN AFRICAN ROAD

1. Peugeot manufacturing figures provided by Peugeot Nigeria, Ltd. I toured their Kaduna plant in March 1993.

2. Antoine de Saint Exupéry, *Night Flight* (New York: Harcourt Brace Jovanovich, 1932), 12–13.

WAITING FOR THE MARABOUT

1. Robert Charlick, *Niger: Personal Rule and Survival in the Sahel* (Boulder: Westview Press, 1991), 11.

2. V. S. Naipaul, "The Crocodiles of Yamoussoukro," in *Finding the Center* (London: Andre Deutsch, 1984), 175.

3. *Haské* (Niamey, Niger), April 1, 1993.

4. Bonkano testimony quotes come from cassette recordings of Bonkano's testimony before Niger's Commission of Crimes and Abuses, Niamey, 1991.

5. From Lieutenant Mathey's July 1944 political report on Zinder, in the Zinder file, Archives Nationale, Niamey.

6. Keletigui Mariko, *Le monde mystérieux des chasseurs traditionnels* (Dakar: Les Nouvelles Editions Africaines, in association with the French Agence de Cooperation Culturelle et Technique, 1981), 10. English translations are mine.

7. Mariko's poem "Mysteriéuse Afrique" appears in his collection of

poems entitled *Poèmes sahéliens en liberté* (Paris: La Pensée Universelle, 1987), 23.

ZINDER NOTES

1. Saint Exupéry, *Night Flight*, 41–42.
2. Historical records in Zinder's provincial archives confirm de Gaulle's visit on February 2, 1944. De Gaulle was on a tour of Free French colonies following a conference of Free French representatives in Brazzaville, Congo. I gathered details of his visit from surviving eyewitnesses, particularly the *griot* Mazo dan Alalo.
3. I heard Mazo sing the Bodout song in Zinder and bought a cassette recording of the song. My friend Mahamane Bandya—a Zinder singer— helped me translate Mazo's work.

DRIVING TO MADNESS

1. The World Bank economist is Michel Guillaud, whom I interviewed in Abidjan in April 1993.
2. Howard French, "West Africans Find Prosperity Is Elusive," *New York Times*, April 9, 1995.
3. Chinua Achebe quotes are from his novel, *Anthills of the Savannah* (New York: Doubleday, 1987), 194, 199.

LISTENING TO MARIKO

1. Klobb and Meynier quotes are from their combined journals, published as *A la recherche de Voulet* (Paris: Nouvelles Éditions Argot, 1931), 147–49. I consulted two sources for details of the Central African Mission story: the Klobb-Meynier journals and the official French records of the story in the Central African Mission file at the Archives Nationale in Niamey. The file contains eyewitness accounts of several officers who investigated the mission's atrocities and the testimony of officers who survived the mission.
2. Maurice Abadie, *La colonie du Niger* (Paris: Société d'Éditions Géographiques, Maritimes et Colonials, Ancienne Maison Challamel, 1927), 315–16.

3. *A la recherche de Voulet*, 129.

4. From a personal letter Klobb wrote from the field, dated June 11, 1899, to an addressee named Binger. A copy of the letter is in the Central African Mission file in the Archives Nationale, Niamey.

5. Keletigui Mariko, "Afrique sans frontières," in Mariko, *Poèmes sahéliens en liberté*, 20.

6. Keletigui Mariko, *Souvenirs de la boucle du Niger* (Dakar: Nouvelles Éditions Africaine, 1977), 178.

7. The Klobb and Voulet portraits are in Jacques-Francis Rolland, *Le grand capitaine* (Paris: Éditions Grasset et Fasquelle, 1976).

8. From Granderye's March 1, 1899, political report, Central African Mission file, Archives Nationale, Niamey.

9. I pieced together what the Central African Mission might have looked like from the mission's records in the Archives Nationale, Niamey. The records detail the expedition's size, the supplies it carried, and its itinerary. I also consulted *A la recherche de Voulet* and Rolland's book, *Le grand capitaine*. Finally, I traveled the territory myself, alone and with Keletigui Mariko, whose father served in Lieutenant Colonel Klobb's detachment assigned to hunt Captain Voulet.

10. Copies of Voulet's letters to Klobb are available in the Central African Mission file in the Archives Nationale, Niamey. Voulet's field reports—copies and some originals—are also in the file.

11. The *dossier de l'enquête*, the French military's official investigation of the Central African Mission's atrocities and Klobb's murder, was released on October 4, 1901. A copy is in the Central African Mission file, Archives Nationale, Niamey.

12. The references to *la soudanité* and *le cafard* come from the anonymous introduction to the Klobb-Meynier journals, *A la recherche de Voulet*, 16. During my travels I found that the terms are still popular with French aid workers, diplomats, and military personnel.

A WOMAN AT THE WHEEL

1. World Bank statistics and quote are from John D. N. Riverson and Steve Carapetis, "Intermediate Means of Transport in Sub-Saharan Af-

rica," Africa Technical Department Series, Technical Paper 161 (Washington, D.C.: World Bank, 1991), 10–11.

2. Mary Smith, *Baba of Karo* (New York: Praeger, 1964), 54–55.

3. Rolland, *Le grand capitaine*, 14.

4. *A la recherche de Voulet*, 123.

5. Abdoulaye Mamani, *Sarraounia* (Paris: Éditions l'Harm A Woman at the Wheel attan, Collection Encres noires, 1992), 33.

Bibliographical Essay

This book is the product of years of intensive road time, but it also reflects a great deal of reading and months spent in libraries and bookstores in Africa; Paris; Washington, D.C.; and at Pennsylvania State University's Pattee Library. I read hundreds of books and documents and have tried to reveal in this narrative the books that helped and inspired me most.

During my travels and the time I spent writing, I returned again and again to firsthand sources, particularly the combined journals of Lieutenant Colonel Jean François Klobb and his adjutant, Lieutenant Octave Meynier. Published under the title *A la recherche de Voulet* (Paris: Nouvelles Éditions Argo, 1931), the journals have been out of print since the 1930s, but Keletigui Mariko lent me a copy he bought at a bookshop in Paris in the 1980s. On my way back to the States in 1993, I hunted through the bookstores of Paris, especially the used book stalls along the Seine River. In one, I found a copy of *l'Afrique noire* (Paris: Bibliothèque de Philosophie Scientifique) published in 1911 by Meynier, who, as a captain, wrote the book as an introductory text for cadets at Saint Cyr, the French military academy.

I also read many expedition journals by British and French explorers, but I found the German explorer Heinrich Barth's *Travels and Discoveries in North and Central Africa* (London: Frank Cass, 1965) to be helpful for his descriptions of the landscape and weather. The journals of the English explorer James Richardson (*Narrative of a Mission to Central Africa 1850–51* [London: Frank Cass, 1970]), who died near Zinder in 1851, were equally valuable.

The French government report entitled *La colonie du Niger* (Paris: Société d'Éditions Géographiques, Maritimes et Colonials, Ancienne Maison Challamel, 1927), by Maurice Abadie, can probably be found only in France's Bibliothèque Nationale in Paris or in the government archives. I borrowed a copy from Keletigui Mariko's personal library.

The other colonial documents, such as Captain Granderye's Rapport politique (Say, Niger, March 1, 1899) or the military Dossier de l'enquête on the Central African Mission (Dakar, October 4, 1901), must be read in the national archives of Niger or in France's colonial archives.

Finally, the oral history of a Hausa woman, *Baba of Karo* (New York: Praeger, 1964), recorded by the English anthropologist Mary Smith, helped me complete the most difficult research task of this book, a profile of an African woman commercial driver.

AFRICAN WRITERS

The poetry, fiction, and memoirs of many African writers influenced my thinking. Among them I read Abdoulaye Mamani's *Sarraounia* (Paris: Éditions l'Harmattan, 1992), which, in the guise of fiction, offers an excellent account of the Central African Mission from an African point of view. Keletigui Mariko's memoir, *Souvenirs de la boucle du Niger* (Dakar: Nouvelles Éditions Africaines, 1977), gave me some insight into his personality and thinking. I read as well his anthropological study of traditional hunters, *Le monde mystérieux des chasseurs traditionnels* (Paris: Nouvelles Éditions Africaines, with the French Agence de Cooperation Culturelle et Technique, 1981). His poetry collection, *Poèmes sahéliens en liberté* (Paris: La Pensée Universelle, 1987), helped my understanding of the spirituality of African life.

The Nigerian writer Ben Okri's Booker Prize–winning novel, *The Famished Road* (London: Safari Books, 1991), formed an important part of my early education about African road lore, as did much of the poetry of his countryman Wole Soyinka, who won the 1986 Nobel Prize for literature and has written extensively—poetry, plays, fiction, and essays—on Ogun, the Yoruba deity of iron and the road. I'm thinking in particular of Soyinka's play *The Road* (London: Oxford University Press, 1973), which explores the world of the motor park and the road in Nigeria. Also, Soyinka's poetry collection, *Idanre* (London: Methuen, 1967), includes five poems of the road, including "Death in the Dawn," which opens:

Traveller, you must set out
At dawn. And wipe your feet upon
The dog-nose wetness of earth.

A novel by a third Nigerian writer, Chinua Achebe, helped confirm my fears and ideas about Africa's road checkpoints. This book, *Anthills of the Savannah* (New York: Doubleday, 1987), climaxes with a bitter road confrontation that crystallized with disturbing clarity in my mind.

I'm indebted as well to a childhood literary companion, Graham Greene, who wrote *Journey without Maps* (Middlesex, England: Penguin Books, 1971), a story that piqued my interest in Africa as a teenager. Two other books, *Night Flight* (New York: Harcourt Brace Jovanovich, 1932) and *Wind, Sand and Stars* (London: Penguin Books, 1995), by the French aviator and writer Antoine de Saint-Exupéry, provided me with a context for understanding bush taxi drivers against the background of modern Africa. Finally, V. S. Naipaul's essay, "Crocodiles of Yamoussoukro," published in his collection, *Finding the Center* (London: Andre Deutsch, 1984), offers an insightful and skeptical view of African spiritual beliefs.

HISTORICAL SOURCES

I read many histories: various accounts of political rule in Africa, of colonial explorations and attempts to govern, of the continent's environmental history, and of the various economic experiments of Africa's independence. But I found little on the Central African Mission. Two books are very important: Douglas Porch's *The Conquest of the Sahara* (New York: Fromm International Publishing, 1986) devotes an entire chapter to the story and offers an excellent overview of France's colonial adventures in West and North Africa; and Jacques-Francis Rolland's *Le grande capitaine* (Paris: Éditions Grasset et Fasquelle, 1976) explores Captain Paul Voulet's adventures in the form of a well-documented historical novel.

Also important for overall history is Robert B. Charlick's *Niger: Personal Rule and Survival in the Sahel* (Boulder, Colo.: Westview Press, 1991), which offers consistent technical background and analyses of Niger's political, economic, and religious evolution since independence in 1961.

SOURCES OF EPIGRAPHS

The quote from Wole Soyinka in the chapter entitled "The Fickle God" I saw posted in the Ibadan, Nigeria, offices of Nigeria's federal Road Safety Commission, which Soyinka founded. The quote was part of a warning to commission officers against taking bribes: "I must . . . warn marshals that those who continue to accept bribes in return for defaulting on their responsibilities are taking Blood Money. One way or another, they will eventually render account. The road is patient, but it does not forgive."

Sources of the other chapter epigraphs are as follows: "The Dogs of the Road," Abadie, *La colonie du Niger;* "A Driver, a Checkpoint, an African Road," Saint Exupéry, *Night Flight;* "Waiting for the Marabout," Okri, *The Famished Road;* "Zinder Notes," Greene, *Journey without Maps;* "Driving to Madness," Wole Soyinka's poem "In Memory of Segun Awolowo," from *Idanre;* "Listening to Mariko" and "A Woman at the Wheel," suras 21 and 4 of the Koran; "An Ugly American," Hausa proverb first uttered to me by a fellow passenger waiting for a bush taxi in Niamey.

TECHNICAL SOURCES

I updated my statistics with information from Niger's Gendarmerie Nationale, which publishes an annual report on road accidents entitled *Rapport sur les accidents de la circulation routière*. I consulted the 1995 and 1996

World Almanacs, and *World Transport Data*, a reference book published annually by the International Road Transport Union in Washington, D.C.

Technical and scientific reports—dry and arrogant as many are in reporting on African issues—gave me background for understanding Africa's troubled road system. Two reports—*Transport Policy Issues in Sub-Saharan Africa*, by Hernan Levy and Patrick O. Malone (Policy Seminar Report 9, Washington, D.C.: World Bank Economic Development Institute, 1988); and *Intermediate Means of Transport in Sub-Saharan Africa*, by John Riverson and Steve Carapetis (Washington, D.C.: World Bank African Technical Department Series, 1991)—provided useful analyses and hard statistics. The World Bank also published *Rural Roads in Sub-Saharan Africa*, by John Riverson, Juan Gaviria, and Sydney Thriscutt (Washington, D.C.: World Bank Africa Technical Department Series, 1991), which offers a very honest, hard overview of Africa's road situation.

I read Richard Barrett's World Bank report, *Urban Transport in West Africa* (Washington, D.C.: World Bank Urban Transport Series, 1990); and *The Road Maintenance Initiative,* by Steve Carapetis, Hernan Levy, and Terje Wolden (Washington, D.C.: World Bank Economic Development Institute, 1991). The African Development Bank's 1988 *Economic Report on Africa* (Abidjan, Ivory Coast: African Development Bank Economic Commission for Africa) offers historical context and more numbers, as does *Trends in Developing Economies* (Washington, D.C.: World Bank, 1995).

I'm grateful to John Riverson of the World Bank for guiding me to the right material, and to Keletigui Mariko, who gave me access to his library and his life.

Index